D - Orudo Brunacci
Assisi 5.09.05

Dear Mary Ann

may this slice of Assisi's history
show you the hope of God!

Pace e bene!
André ofm
&
Josef sfo

Three Heroes of Assisi in World War II

Bishop Giuseppe Nicolini
Colonel Valentin Müller
Don Aldo Brunacci

Edited and written by
Josef Raischl SFO and André Cirino OFM

EDITRICE MINERVA - ASSISI

ISBN 88-87021-73-2

To all
who suffered and still suffer
from persecution and war

Contents

Preface *by Jean François Godet-Calogeras* .... » 8

Introduction *by Josef Raischl and André Cirino* .... » 13

Chronology 1943-1944 .... » 16

Saving Assisi During World War II *by Francesco Santucci*
  1. The German Occupation .... » 18
  2. How Can Assisi Be Saved? .... » 24
  3. Assisi: A Hospital City .... » 42
  4. The Liberation .... » 53

The True Story *by Aldo Brunacci* .... » 59

The Unsung Hero: Bishop Nicolini *by Aldo Brunacci*...... » 66

Assisi Hero *by Susan Saint Sing*................................. » 78

In Assisi Not One Was Touched *by Aldo Brunacci*.......... » 87

From A Courageous Youth of Yesterday *by Mario Spinelli* .. » 92

Jewish Refugees *by Aldo Brunacci* .... » 98

A Personal Note: "Storia Medicinali" *by Bishop Nicolini* . » 102

Dr. Valentin Müller *by Josef Raischl* .... » 103

Colonel Valentin Müller, MD *by André Cirino and Josef Raischl* .... » 107

Remembering Compassion During War *by Candice Hughes* » 114

Footnote to "Assisi Underground" *by Aldo Brunacci* ...... » 117

The Secret Letter *by Delia Gallagher* .... » 120

University Honors Italian Priest for Helping Jews in World
War II .... » 129

Gaudete Medal Awards: St. Bonaventure University *by
Severin Hochberg* .... » 131

Assisi Priest Honored in Washington for Protecting Jews
During World War II *by Gerard Perseghin* .... » 133

Don Aldo Brunacci Discusses His Efforts
To Save 200 Jews During World War II *by Bob Edwards*.. » 137

Assisi, 1943 *by Edward Kislinger* .... » 141

Prayer in House of Representatives *by Aldo Brunacci* ..... » 144

Preface

There is no such thing as a just war. For centuries, men have tried to justify their violence. When needed, they would use God – whatever name they would give God – to bless their armies, weapons, and killings. Throughout history even Christians forgot – and still forget today – that Jesus taught and lived unconditional nonviolence. Violence and war never solved problems or conflicts. When they are over, beyond an illusion of peace, they always generate more violence and other wars. And more victims.

Some sixty years ago, World War II was no exception. It was a war that a series of circumstances had arguably made inevitable, but inevitability is not justice. Because of a few, tens of millions of men and women went through hell, and tens of millions of them never got the luck nor the grace to see the end of it. And those who did never forgot.

History books often attach glory to war. And glory there is, but the real one is not in winning battles, taking over strategic places, and overcoming enemies. The real glory is in the human actions of compassion, care and love at the risk of one's life. Those actions happen and should get more attention than the acts of violence. History ought to be told through the positive actions of the loving, the caring and the peacemaking.

A small city of central Italy has had such glory for centuries: Assisi, the city of Saint Francis, the thirteenth century man who spoke to the birds and tamed a wolf. If the popular image is not wrong, it should not hide the fact that Francis's life is filled with acts of compassion and peace: care for the poor and the outcast, reconciliation between a bishop and a mayor of the city, attempt of nonviolent resolution of a crusade, outreach to those the medieval Christianity considered as the worst enemies, the Muslims. All that because Francis, in his own words, wanted to live according to the Gospel and follow the teachings and the footsteps of Jesus Christ.

Over sixty years ago, in 1943-1944, amidst the horrors of the most murderous conflict in human history, Assisi had another time of true glory. While the Allies had just landed in Sicily and with great difficulty were progressing north from southern Italy, Assisi was occupied by German troops. There, two men worked together to do something constructive rather than destructive: the bishop of Assisi, Monsignor Giuseppe Nicolini, and the German officer in command, a medical doctor from Bavaria, Colonel Valentin Müller. Divided by the war opposing their countries, the two men remained nevertheless united by their Christian faith and its mandate of unconditional love. They obtained that Assisi be made hospital city, a city for medical care, not for military confrontation; a city for healing, not for fighting.

A little later, another positive action was started, this time with the participation of a third local hero. Bishop Nicolini received a letter from the Secretariat of State of the Vatican urging him to provide aid for the growing number of Jewish refugees fleeing the Nazi persecution. The bishop asked his secretary to help him create and develop the underground network that would shelter and save, without the knowledge of the German occupants, more than two hundred Jews coming from various regions of Europe. The secretary was Don Aldo Brunacci, who was barely thirty years old at the time.

This book relates the story of what happened, thanks to those three men, and how, because they were human beings in distress, Jews were rescued by caring Christians that war had officially made enemies. Obviously, Colonel Müller was never informed or made an accomplice of the rescue of the

Colonel Valentin Müller (1891-1951)

Jews: it would have made him a traitor, and would have most certainly compromised the whole operation. Everything had to remain underground. But Colonel Müller's humanitarian acts and decisions did help, and one might think that, intelligent as he was, he had intuited what was going on in the Umbrian city in those days. His repeated interventions against ruthless SS and Gestapo members were certainly and clearly in favor of the oppressed.

Today, Don Aldo Brunacci is the last survivor of that trio of beautiful heroes. And prefacing this book gives me an opportunity to celebrate the bond of friendship that has grown for more than thirty years, since those days of October 1974 when I first came to Assisi for a conference of the International Society of Franciscan Studies of which Don Aldo was an active member, being a recognized scholar himself. Many times Don Aldo has told the story of what happened in Assisi during World War II. And he is a lively, passionate story teller. But always does he praise the courageous action of Bishop Nicolini, Colonel Müller, and the good Assisian people who helped; always does he remember how those Jewish families became his friends. Very often—I witnessed it several times—Don Aldo would be asked the question: why? Why did you risk your life for some Jews, for some people who were not Christian? Don Aldo's answer is always the same, simple and clear, unpretentious and self-explanatory: Because that is what the Gospel asks a Christian to do. The unconditional mandate of love so well illustrated in the parable of the Good Samaritan.

What happened in Assisi sixty years ago remains an inspiration for us today, in our not-so-peaceful world. What happened then shows what happens when human beings put their true and deep beliefs into practice, no matter what; when human beings put their faith and love above any other worldly loyalty. Obedience to God comes before obedience to men, the early disciples of Christ used to say. Bishop Nicolini, Colonel Müller, and Don Aldo Brunacci did not do anything less in the city of Saint Francis, the brother and the peacemaker. And it is for good reason that until today, as the authentic Assisian he is, Don Aldo likes to say, with a blend of humility and pride, that he is *un francescano di cuore*, a Franciscan at heart. Through his deeds, he certainly showed how truly he is.

Jean François Godet-Calogeras, Ph.D.
Associate Professor, School of Franciscan Studies
St. Bonaventure University

Introduction

War knows no beauty and recognizes no art. It is a question of life and death, of victory and defeat. Destruction and devastation are its inevitable consequences. Soldiers can only show mercy and compassion in thinking of their homeland. What good are guarantees? What is the use of neutral zones? Military advantage is the first rule of war in every age.

On 11 May 1944 the Benedictine Abbey of Montecassino shared in the destiny of destruction in war. Centuries of art and culture were reduced to dust in minutes. Assisi – that Umbrian town filled with historical art and monuments dear to the spirituality of millions of people – could have suffered a similar fate. Assisi's survival is no accident.

People look for things to do, and that includes good things as well. In the midst of every crisis and conflict there are stout-hearted people who are signs of hope in the midst of anguish and doubt. Individuals have put all kinds of plans into motion, have kept cool heads and used every bit of their creativity and determination without losing sight of values such as beauty, justice and unity.

That is what this book is meant to recall. Amidst all the horrible things that happened, its purpose is to document the good things that happened. Unfortunately, that is not what happened in the case of the film by Dr. Alexander Ramati, *Assisi Underground* (1984).

In spite of the thoroughly researched and well-documented work of Francesco Santucci – *Assisi 1943-1944, Documenti Per Una Storia* – Assisi today, even with contributions from many eye-witnesses, cannot compete with the excitement and popularity of a film. For this reason we have chosen to translate and publish these extracts in the hope that it may help us to focus on real persons and events. Doubtless, Francis of Assisi was one of those real persons, as was Clare. And many people followed in their footsteps and discovered new ways of living their life according to the Gospel of Jesus.

Today, too, real people need our attention and solidarity. And we and our world need these real people, as real as the three heroes[1] described in this little book: Bishop Giuseppe Placido Nicolini, Bishop of Assisi until his death in 1973; Colonel Valentin Müller, MD Commander of the city of Assisi from September 1943 to June 1944 (†1951); Don[2] Aldo Brunacci, (born 1913) the last surviving witness. We are especially grateful for the gift of his life and for his simple yet powerful presence in Assisi.

Both of us travelled to Assisi in 1987 as part of a study week in conjunction with the Institute for Franciscan Spirituality at the *Antonianum* in Rome. We lodged just across the road from the Bishop's ancient palace at Santa Maria Maggiore. André already knew Don Aldo Brunacci by then, and Josef was poised to marry the grand-daughter of Colonel Valentin Müller, Bernadette Müller. So both of us connected early-on with the history of this holy place. Finally, in 1999, in order to report more accurately on the facts concerning Assisi during the war years 1943-44, we decided to translate a portion of Santucci's work. Josef was in close contact with his wife's family and André spent several months each year at Casa Papa Giovanni with Don Aldo Brunacci. So the book grew out of this backdrop.

---

[1] We chose the word "hero" to describe these three protagonists not only because we see them as heroes, but also because some contributors to this book have actually called them heroes. Cf. pp. 66, 67, 78, 83, 93, 108.

[2] The word "Don" is a title used for Italian priests, much the same way English-speakers may use "Father" or "Reverend."

We are aware of many repetitions in the accounts of these historical events, and we decided not to edit them out so that the story becomes more familiar to us, even part of us. In the accounts we have chosen, some facts, at times very minor, may vary such as the number of Jewish people saved. This latter fact remains inaccurate because, as Don Aldo told us, records of names were not kept so as to protect the absorption of the Jews into the city population and "prudence dictated that nothing should be written down."[3]

We would like to thank all those people who helped make this book possible and encouraged us, especially all who graciously gave us reprint permissions for material chosen for this book. We express our gratitude to Professor Francesco Santucci, the author of the basic historical work, who agreed to the translation of some excerpts. We are grateful to Sister Nancy Celaschi, a Franciscan from the USA, who translated Santucci's text. We would also like to thank Dr. Valentin Müller's family, especially his two children, Dr. Irmgard Heinemann and Dr. Robert Müller for their recollections. Our gratitude to Jean-François Godet-Calogeras for graciously contributing the preface to this work. Finally, Don Aldo Brunacci who was not merely an eyewitness but was intimately involved in these events and contributed some of his own recollections. He is not simply an author, but an actor in these historical events. We hope that we have fulfilled his desire to "publish all the documents in my possession regarding the events in question... I hope to do this as soon as possible, because only the truth deserves to be known."[4]

Josef Raischl SFO and André Cirino OFM
Dachau/New York, Easter 2005

---

[3] See p. 69.
[4] See p. 119.

Historical overview[1]

1943

25 July   Fascism is overthrown in Italy. Mussolini is captured.

September   British and American troops land in southern Italy. German and Italian troops fight the Allies and the Italian Resistance.

9 September   The Germans occupy Assisi.

Mid-September Benito Mussolini is freed by the Germans and proclaims the *Repubblica Sociale Italiana*.

16 October   The Germans begin their purge of the Jewish ghetto in Rome.

30 October   Allied planes bomb the Sant' Egidio Airport near Assisi.

---

[1] Santucci, pp. 299-304. Used with permission.

1944

7 January	Seventeen Assisians die in the bombardment of Sant'Egidio.
1 March	Dr. Müller is named commander of the German troops in Assisi.
11 May	The Abbey of Montecassino is bombed and completely destroyed.
31 May	General Kesselring, Supreme Commander of German troops in Italy, agrees to declare Assisi a hospital city.
4 June	Rome is liberated by the Allied troops.
16 June	German troops, together with the wounded, leave Assisi.
17 June	The Allies establish a new municipal government in Assisi.
31 August	By agreement of the Vatican, the Bishop of Assisi and the army command, Assisi is to be kept free of troops and military exercises.

THE GERMAN OCCUPATION OF ASSISI[1]

8 September 1943 – 16 June 1944

The Arrival of the First German Divisions

After 8 September 1943 the first Germans arrived in Assisi, "driving the rich people out of the Subasio, Giotto and Savoia Hotels."[2] Only a few days before the cease-fire an Italian-German meeting was held in the holy city. Officially it was about economic matters, but in reality it dealt with military questions. The meeting was held in the Hotel Subasio. At that time there were rumors of greater military developments in Assisi. On 8 September a German captain on an exploration trip entered the courtyard of the Sacro Convento in a truck, carrying a hand grenade and automatic weapon to subject the Custos "to a relentless interrogation on various topics."[3]

During the first few days of October 1943 the Germans occupied the city with some troops from the airborne forces and military medical corps. The former, who worked at the nearby Sant'Egidio airfield, were lodged at the Subasio Hotel; the latter were billeted at the former Italian convalescent home

---

[1] Santucci, pp. 35-51, *Occupazione tedesca della città.* Used with permission. English translation by Nancy Celaschi OSF.

[2] Cf. B. Mansi, *Relazione circa alcune particolari attività dei Frati Minori Conventuali di Assisi durante la presente guerra,* 12 August 1944, Archives of the Sacro Convento, *b. Santa Sede-Telegrammi, Rescritti, Decreti,* typewritten manuscript, p. 9.

[3] Ibid., p. 10.

(today the Seraphic Institute) to establish the first German field hospital (*Feld Lazarett*) in Assisi.[4]

After 8 September 1943 the Locatelli Palace[5] was designated to house the German military wounded. It served in this capacity until 16 June 1944. (Beginning on 17 June 1944 it would house Allied soldiers and partisan formations)[6].

A second hospital was established several days later in the buildings of the Prince of Naples National Home for Orphans of Teachers:

> On 10 October, with absolutely no warning, German forces occupied the whole complex, except for the palazzina... and the 29 orphans were left to live and study in those few rooms. The main building was transformed first into a reception center for the wounded and, immediately after that, into a military hospital.
>
> The living situation shared by the personnel of the home and the German military was proper, marked by mutual respect. There were cordial relations between the rector and the German Commander who, often commiserating with the conditions under which the people of the home were forced to live, ordered those under him to give the children medicine, school supplies and even food.

That year the Franciscan celebrations of 3-4 October were still held, but somewhat toned down.

---

[4] Cf. B. Calzolari, *L'Hotel Subasio specchio dei tempi Momenti di vita assisana dal 1868 in poi*, Assisi, Tip. Porziuncola, 1983, p. 157. The only representative of the Italian army in Assisi was Colonel Guido Manardi, later general of the Monte Rosa division, who took the initiative of creating a "Presidium command" (composed of himself) in Assisi, thus permitting the Germans to have an interlocutor in the city. (ibid.)

[5] Editors' footnote: Now Casa Papa Giovanni.

[6] Information received from Rev. Otello Migliosi.

National Home for Orphans of Teachers, Center of the second German military hospital in Assisi

Those first German divisions quickly revealed their arrogance and violence. Bearing witness to this was, among others, the Mayor of Assisi at that time, Arnaldo Fortini, who said:

> One evening their commander, a captain of the Luftwaffe, called me to the Hotel Savoia where he was staying, and through an interpreter informed me of many bans to be imposed on the people, almost all of which were punishable by death-execution for whoever did not turn in their arms, for anyone committing sabotage, for anyone who perpetrated any activity against the German military, for anyone found in certain areas, etc. At the end he asked me for a certain number of hostages, to be taken from the more suspect elements.
>
> I replied that no Italian could possibly agree to such a request and hand other Italians over to a foreign army, regardless of which army it may be, without bringing great shame upon himself. And since that captain insisted, I added that

if he were in my place and under the same conditions, he would certainly have acted in the same way.

This calm but decisive statement seemed to have touched him. He replied that he appreciated my position and he was willing to renounce the idea of the hostages, on the condition that I would accept personal responsibility for whatever might occur. I agreed without hesitation; and thus it came about that not a single citizen of Assisi was deported, not a single one was executed or taken in reprisal.

On 15 October the Germans requisitioned the Theological College of the Friars Minor Conventual, menacingly asking the rector to hand over the keys to some storage areas immediately.[7] At three o'clock the following afternoon, German officers and soldiers, led by a Gestapo officer, surrounded the Basilica of St. Francis and the Sacro Convento, blocking the exits, in order to check all the religious to see if there were any English or American soldiers hidden there.

They conducted "a thorough search of the whole convent. Entering part of the complex reserved to the sisters, the search teams found two articles of men's clothing and threatened the sisters with deportation to Germany and accusation before a military tribunal."[8] In reality they were clothes belonging to two men who worked in the convent gardens, as was proven by papers found in the pockets.[9]

After this awful experience the Custos hurriedly sent one of his confreres to Rome the following day, 17 October, "to inform the Father General of the search by the Germans and to ask the Holy See for a document of exemption from search and seizure."[10] On that same day, at the same hour as the day

---

[7] Cf. Mansi, *Relazione*, p. 10.

[8] Cf. Mansi, p. 10.

[9] Cf. P.S. Attal, *Assisi città santa. Come fu salvata dagli orrori della guerra*, in MISCELLANEA FRANCESCANA, 48 (948) I, pp. 11-12.

[10] *Chronicle of the Sacro Convento.*

The first Allied troops enter the Piazza del Comune, morning of 17 June 1944

before, some German officers searched the Sacro Convento a second time, interrogating and studying the documents of all the foreign religious. This two-day investigation ended without incident, but "the whole city" was surprised "about the illegal action taken against the Basilica and the Sacro Convento, which are the property of the Holy See."[11]

On 19 October the governor of Vatican City, Marquis Serafini, was charged by the Secretary of State, Cardinal Luigi Maglione, to present to the German Military Authorities in Italy a document certifying that the Basilica and the buildings connected to it were the property of the Holy See and, as such, were exempt from any search or seizure.[12]

On 18 November the Apostolic Nuncio in Italy, Archbishop Francesco Borgongini Duca, sent Fr. Bede Hess, General Minister of the Friars Minor Conventual, the official declaration of the Holy See, confirmed by the German Military Authority, concerning the accord[13] on the basis of which the following notices could be posted to the doors of the Basilica, the Sacro Convento and other buildings belonging to them: "Proprietà della S. Sede. ESENTE. Eigentum des Heiligen Stuhles."[14]

However, saving Assisi from war and destruction was an entirely different matter. The religious and civil authorities had been working on this matter for some time.

---

[11] Ibid.

[12] Ibid.

[13] Cf. Attal, p. 12.

[14] Ibid. and *Chronicle of the Sacro Convento*. Trans. note: The signs declared, in Italian and German, "Property of the Holy See. Exempt."

HOW TO SAVE ASSISI[1]

In a brief analysis, one realizes that there were five persons especially involved in the effort to save the city of Assisi:

- the General Minister of the Friars Minor Conventual, Fr. Bede Hess;
- the Custos of the Sacro Convento, Fr. Bonaventura Mansi;
- the Bishop of Assisi, Bishop Giuseppe Placido Nicolini;
- the Mayor of Assisi, Arnaldo Fortini;
- the director of the German military hospitals in Assisi, Colonel Valentin Müller, MD

Although we know what would eventually be done to save Assisi would be the result of their joint effort and harmony, down to this very day it is difficult to state for certain which of these men made the first move, initiating the long, patient, tenacious and ultimately successful process. On this subject, Francesco Salvatore Attal writes:

> Early in 1941 the Custos of the Sacro Convento, Fr. Bonaventure Mansi OFM Conv., spoke to the Mayor of Assisi, Arnaldo Fortini, concerning the danger the city faced because of the presence in various places – including the Sala Norsa very near the Sacro Convento and dependent on it – of Italian recruits in training. This situation could result in some dangerous development by turning the city into an

---

[1] Santucci, pp. 51-70, *Come salvare Assisi*. Used with permission. English translation by Nancy Celaschi OSF.

active military center, exposing it to the risks of war. Arnaldo Fortini, who had been administering the city astutely and with steadfast dedication, immediately understood what the Custos meant. Bishop Placido Nicolini, the well-loved ordinary, was informed of the situation as well and gave his full support to the initiatives being planned.

They decided to approach the Italian authorities and insist that the recruits be removed, and institute instead a military convalescent hospital in Assisi. Also making a contribution to the success of the project was the late Colonel Alfred Baduel, MD, Director of the Hospital of Assisi. Thus, to the agreement of all, the convalescent hospital was opened at the Institute for the Blind and Deaf, just outside of Porta San Francesco. The Bishop sent the Sisters of St. Mary of the Angels there and appointed a chaplain. Thus the first danger was averted and no fighting divisions were lodged in Assisi.[2]

Arnaldo Fortini recalls the following:

On Easter Monday 1942, while the people of Assisi were rendering their traditional homage of the veil of the Blessed Virgin who throughout the centuries had preserved the city from so many afflictions, in my capacity as Mayor of the city and President of the International Society of Franciscan Studies, I suggested to Fr Giuseppe Abate, himself a member of the same society and General Secretary of the Order of Friars Minor Conventual, the undertaking of direct action to save Assisi from conflict and destruction of war, confident that I was expressing the desire of peoples of all nations. This suggestion was also shared with the Custos of the Sacro Convento, Fr. Bonaventura Mansi.

We had to overcome some very serious obstacles which arose because of our status as citizens of one of the countries at war, thus forbidden to have relations not only with the hostile states, but with neutral ones as well. Consequently we turned to Fr. Bede Hess, General Minister of the Friars Minor

---

[2] Attal, pp. 4-5.

Detail of the tombstone of Col, Valentin Müller, depicting the Basilica of St. Francis and the Sacro Convento

Conventual, who took the required steps to approach the Secretariat of State of the Holy See...[3]

Recalling the steps taken to safeguard Assisi, at the end of 1944 Bishop Nicolini in a memo sent to the military governor of the city, Lieutenant Garigue, stated: "First of all, the Custos of the Convento of San Francesco, encouraged by me, asked the Holy See to urge the ambassadors of the various nations at war to take an interest."[4]

However, it would be good to follow step by step the long journey of this cause, relying most of all on the documents available to us.[5]

---

[3] Fortini, p. 215. See also the BOLLETINO DELLA SOCIETÀ INTERNAZIONALE DI STUDI FRANCESCANI, 1946, fasc. XIV -XV -XVI, pp. 61-62.

[4] Diocesan Archives of Assisi, Bishop Nicolini, autograph ms.

[5] These documents are preserved in the archives of the Vatican Secretariat of State and that of the Order of Friars Minor Conventual in Rome which I

Before studying the action taken through the Holy See and, through this action, appealing to the diplomatic or military representatives of the warring nations – and even to the heads of state of some of them – it should be noted that as early as 16 July 1943 the Franciscans at the Sacro Convento in Assisi, were concerned about protecting the tomb of St. Francis from any eventual damage caused by the advancing war. Therefore, they appealed to the Pope for authorization, asking him also to forbid the construction of an underground chamber near the Basilica, which the civic authorities were planning for use as an air raid shelter.[6]

On 4 August the Apostolic Nuncio in Italy, Archbishop Francesco Borgongini Duca, replied: "The Holy Father had kindly deigned to grant the authorization for the work planned for the protection of the venerated tomb of the Seraphic Father" and he would also appeal to the Italian government to construct the chamber elsewhere.[7]

The next day Fr. Mansi left for Rome, summoned by the General Minister of the Order concerning the planned work, and on 6 August the same Minister informed the Nuncio that the Custos was in charge of preparing the plans for the protection of the saint's tomb. The work was entrusted to the architect, Mr. Ugo Tarchi.[8]

It should be pointed out here that the General Minister of the Order of Friars Minor Conventual was an American and had a personal acquaintance with the personal representative of the President of the United States of America to the Holy

---

consulted through published citations, as well as the Diocesan Archives of Assisi and the Archives of the Sacro Convento, which I consulted directly.

[6] Cf. Mansi, p. 9.

[7] Cf. Attal, pp. 8-9. Meanwhile, the air raid shelter was never built.

[8] *Chronicle of the Sacro Convento.*

See, Mr. Myron C. Taylor, and knew the chargé d'affaires, Mr. Harold H. Tittmann, even better.[9]

It was to the latter gentleman that, on 7 August 1943, Fr. Bede Hess gave an explanatory document in which he asked the United States government to intervene so that the Basilica of St. Francis and the whole city of Assisi might be saved from "ground or air attack."[10]

The official letter of Fr. Bede Hess ended as follows:

> As General Superior of the Franciscan Order of Friars Minor Conventual to whom the care of the Sacred Basilica is entrusted, in the name of all the followers and admirers of St. Francis and as an American citizen who, next to God, passionately loves his country, I strongly ask you to request our government to issue an order to our ground and air forces that the Sacred Basilica of St. Francis of Assisi should be saved for its historical, architectural and artistic value, because it is papal property in the custody of my Order, because it is an object of affection and veneration for millions of followers and admirers of the Saint including the United States of America, and because there are no military installations in Assisi.[11]

However, the Custos of the Basilica did not let up, and while the General Minister was in Assisi from 13-18 August, he informed Fr. Hess that there was continued danger of a "militarization of Assisi as an arms and munitions depot." He asked him to notify the Holy See so that such a threat would be removed far from the city.[12]

In the interim, Mr. Tarchi had drawn up plans for protecting the tomb of St Francis and on 25 August the Custos sent them to Italy's Minister of Public Works. However, Min-

---

[9] Cf. Attal, p. 9.
[10] Cf. *Chronicle of the Sacro Convento.*
[11] Attal, p. 9.
[12] *Chronicle of the Sacro Convento.*

Bishop Giuseppe Placido Nicolini

ister Allicata informed him that, following upon the events of 25 July, all work on the Sacro Convento was suspended.[13]

On 2 September the Vatican Secretariat of State replied to the requests and concerns expressed by Fr. Bede Hess, stating that the "fear of military measures (planned) for Assisi" was "absolutely groundless."[14]

Concerning the tunnel to be excavated next to St. Francis Basilica, the Vatican Secretariat of State on 9 September informed the Father General that the Minister of the Interior had instructed the Prefect of Perugia to "suspend all plans regarding the construction of a tunnel in Assisi, which was to be dug in the territory of the Sacro Convento."[15]

In early autumn 1943, as we have already noted, a German military hospital was opened in Assisi. On 3 November the new head of the Province of Perugia, Dr. Armando Rocchi, notified the Military Regional Command and the Mayors about this in a note which stated: "The German Command of Piazza di Perugia has stipulated that, following the preparation of a German field hospital in Assisi, the sick or wounded German soldiers can no longer be admitted to Italian civil and military hospitals."[16]

On 4 December 1943 the Holy See began the paper work to have Assisi recognized and declared as a "hospital city, the only way to save the whole city from the horrors of the war."[17]

On the basis of the suggestions offered by Fr. Mansi, Fr. Bede Hess presented to the Cardinal Secretary of State "a detailed explanation with particular information" regarding the war situation "which was being determined in Assisi."[18]

---

[13] Ibid.

[14] Ibid.

[15] Ibid.

[16] No. 8917 of the Cabinet of the Prefecture of Perugia.

[17] *Chronicle of the Sacro Convento.*

[18] Ibid.

Since this document is of fundamental importance, it would be good to quote the text almost in its entirety:[19]

Two German military hospitals have been established in Assisi, one in the Prince of Naples Home and the other in the new buildings of the Institute for the Deaf, Dumb and Blind, quite near the Basilica. Other buildings in various parts of the city complete the hospital structure. The Subasio, Giotto and Savoia Hotels, all very near the Basilica, house German officers and troops. The airfields of Foligno and Perugia, the latter just a few kilometers from Assisi, have already been affected by recent fighting.

Airplanes from both sides continually fly over Assisi, striking the surrounding areas. There is real justification for concern about preserving the artistic, historic and religious patrimony of the Basilica and the whole city of Assisi. Any damage to this heritage would be an irreparable loss and would be deplored by the whole civilized world which loves the city of St. Francis as a symbol of peace and love, recognizing its absolute lack of military purpose.

Therefore the same measures should be adopted for Assisi as have been adopted for Florence. From an artistic and historical viewpoint alone, functionaries of the Ministry for National Education, with specific functions, have made the first contacts with German military authorities, who have demonstrated their willingness to pass on to their High Command the reasons for preserving Assisi from eventual damage in the war.

I therefore ask Your Eminence to look into the possibility of a diplomatic initiative on the part of the Secretariat of State of the Supreme Pontiff, Pius XII, with the ambassadors of Germany, England and the United States of America, so that the whole city of Assisi may be preserved from wartime harm by all of the armies in battle. If the action of the Ministers of National Education has been considered just and opportune and kindly received because of the care and con-

---

[19] Attal, pp. 12-14.

servation of the vast, priceless, historic, artistic patrimony of the city of Assisi, we trust that the action of the supreme ecclesiastical authority will meet with the highest consideration because of the spiritual importance and the sacred character of the Seraphic City. With such a wealth of religious memorials and shrines, it is venerated throughout the Catholic world and visited by persons of every nation and religion.

Let it also be noted that the Basilica and the Sacro Convento and the related buildings situated in various parts of the city of Assisi are the property of the Holy See, recognized as such by the Concordat of 11 February 1929. Only a commitment agreed upon by all the authorities of the parties at war can save the city of St. Francis from the damage and destruction of the war and fulfill the commitment already undertaken by the German military authorities to respect the property of the Holy See in Assisi.

Since it is held that the presence of two German hospitals in Assisi does not constitute an obstacle to an agreement between the various parties at war, with the city being used for purposes of a medical nature, all that is required is for the various parties to agree to keep the city of Assisi free from military commands of active troops, temporary military commands and passing troops, from storage of arms and military materiel, from artillery or antiaircraft emplacements, from stationing of troops and from offensive or defensive lines, and of any type of military action which leads to damage, devastation, fire or looting.

Such provisions would avert direct offensives. However, it would also be necessary to ensure that any zone of military operations which would eventually be established would be at such a distance as to prevent indirect damage caused by collapse or destruction which can happen so easily due to displacement of air in centuries-old buildings, especially the Basilica, which is built on the side of a geologically faulted hill and has already been subject to many serious fissures.

Bowing to offer you homage,
Fr. Bede M. Hess OFM Conv.
General Minister

After this memo, Fr. Bede sent some informational material, the most significant of which reads as follows:[20]

1. In addition to the two German military hospitals, other buildings have been requisitioned and occupied in various parts of the city so that Assisi is taking on an increasingly military character, the development of which we cannot foresee.

2. Many officials and pilots of the airfield of Perugia, closer to Assisi, are being lodged in the Hotels Subasio, Giotto and Savoia, from which they leave and to which they return after air raids. Such hotels close to the Basilica could draw hostile air bombardment.

3. Squads of workers from Assisi are requisitioned each day and taken to the nearby airfield for military work. The greater effectiveness of the camp itself for defensive action and placement of arms constitutes a serious threat to Assisi.

Added to this was railway and road traffic – almost entirely of a military nature, danger of the possibility of storing munitions in the basement of the military hospitals, searches conducted by the Germans, trouble frequently caused by drunken German soldiers and their numerous threats to blow everything up should they have to retreat so that it could not be used by the enemy.[21]

All this was meant to emphasize the drama of the situation to the Vatican Secretariat of State so that the Holy See might take the necessary measures and avoid even greater risks to Assisi.

On 28 December the General Minister wrote to the Custos of the Sacro Convento, notifying him that the paperwork for the protection of Assisi presented to the Holy See was taking promising turns, but it was necessary for the local civil

---

[20] Ibid., p. 14.
[21] Ibid., pp.14-15.

and military authorities to indicate "the reasons" necessary "for the salvation of Assisi."[22] And so on 4 January 1944 the Custos asked Arnaldo Fortini "to prepare a statement to present to the highest authority in Italy for the protection of Assisi."[23]

In mentioning his own interventions, Fortini would later write that this step was taken upon the initiative of the International Society for Franciscan Studies, which for more than 40 years had its headquarters in Assisi, and of which he had been president for more than 40 years.[24] Fortini writes:[25] "Since we ourselves could not make any direct appeal to Vatican City, it was decided that our official proposal to have Assisi declared an open, hospital city, would be addressed to the government of the Socialist Republic, and that an authenticated copy of this proposal would be sent to the Vatican Secretariat of State."

This did happen, and once again it was Fr. Hess who saw to it that Fortini's letter did arrive at the Secretariat of State.[26]

Concerning this topic, on 20 January 1944 the chronicler of the Sacro Convento noted: "Fortini has prepared the civil statement for the protection of Assisi. The statement is addressed to H.E. Benito Mussolini, Head of the Government of the Italian Socialist Republic."[27] Here follows the complete text of the Mayor's appeal:

---

[22] *Chronicle of the Sacro Convento.*

[23] Ibid. Although retaining the title of Mayor of Assisi, Fortini had de facto been replaced, for reasons of health, by the commissary of the prefecture, Dr. Francesco Paolo Gargiulo. Fortini would resign definitively from the office of Mayor of Assisi on 1 March 1944. On the 12th of the same month the provincial leader, Dr. Armando Rocchi, would name Mr. Alcide Checconi, who would remain in that office until 9 June 1944.

[24] Fortini, p. 216.

[25] Ibid.

[26] Ibid.

[27] Ibid.

In my capacity as Mayor of the city of Assisi[28] and as President of the International Society of Franciscan Studies, I believe it is my duty to submit for your examination the situation in Assisi regarding the unfolding and current operations relating to the war.

Assisi, the heart of the world, is the birthplace of St. Francis and the one city which, after Rome and Jerusalem, because of its tradition of holiness, its artistic treasures and its most noble significance whence Dante was given to salute it as the *Novissimo Oriente*, shines brightly on the heights of the human spirit, but today is threatened by the war which is knocking at its doors.

The wonderful church built over the bodily remains of the Seraphic Saint which a great writer, Adolfo Venturi, called "the most beautiful house of prayer of which the earth can boast," is already caught up in a whirlpool of the battle which, because of frequent aerial bombardments, has already claimed a great number of victims and destroyed important monuments in the surrounding area, from Perugia to Foligno.

And with the famous triple Basilica, immortalized by Cimabue, Giotto and Simone Martini, other Franciscan churches are likewise in danger: San Damiano, the Porziuncola, the Cathedral, the Bishop's house, Santa Maria Sopra Minerva.

It is useless to try to indicate what a loss it would be to people of every nation if any of these masterpieces, not only of art but more so of the spirit, were to be lost!

And indeed, as if by a tacit and instinctive homage to the highest ideals of beauty and goodness which smile upon human hearts, even when they are in mortal combat, the band of iron and fire has reached the threshold of the holy city, over which hundreds of fighter planes fly daily.

We therefore request that, similar to what has happened for Rome, this situation be confirmed de jure, by which the various nations at war would commit themselves or at least

---

[28] Since 1923.

confirm their desire to spare Assisi and the neighboring Franciscan monuments.

It should be kept in mind that the city's fame is of a purely mystical and spiritual nature and that it has absolutely no importance politically (it has only 5,000 inhabitants), industrially (there are no factories within its walls), militarily (there are no forts or troop commands), topographically (it is far from major roads and its rail station, situated on the secondary line from Foligno to Terontola, is five kilometers away from the city).

On the other hand for centuries the faithful from every nation have come on pilgrimage (for the centenary of Francis in 1926 two million visitors from every nation came); the many convents and monasteries (including one monastery each of English, American, Bavarian, Spanish, and French nuns, not to mention the general headquarters of the most flourishing international missionary associations – the Missionaries of Egypt, Gesù Bambino, del Giglio and the Minors Conventual – who have always performed their work in all parts of the world to ease the suffering of people of every country and race); the admiration and veneration of those who love art, from every country, have by now made it an international center of culture and faith, to which all hearts pay homage, without distinction.

Let us note that for more than 40 years the city has been the headquarters of the International Society for Franciscan Studies, founded by the Frenchman Paul Sabatier, and later presided over by the Dane, Joergensen, the Englishman Cuthbert, and today by the undersigned, to which scholars from all nations have given their full participation and collaboration.

Lastly, it should be observed that the Basilica and Sacro Convento of San Francesco (almost one fourth of the whole city), the Conventual Missionary College and the Theological Seminary belong to the Holy See, so that even the German military authorities have already made a direct commitment to the Holy See concerning those buildings to refrain from executing acts of occupation or simple search; that other buildings, such as the Basilica of St. Clare and the Patriarchal Basilica of Saint Mary of the Angels, are under the direct jurisdiction of the Supreme Pontiff.

We ask that opportune measures be taken so that the nations party to the war agree that the Franciscan monuments and the city should be immune from aerial or artillery bombardment, and that there be no offensive or defensive emplacements in it, nor stores of ammunition or military materiel or troop commands, although there could be space for hospitals for the wounded.

Arnaldo Fortini[29]

Indeed, the German army did need other buildings. Thus on 17 January 1944 the German Command asked the Sacro Convento for the complex of the Theological College, located on the Via del Seminario, but received a firm refusal from the Conventuals.[30]

The same building was requested once again as a residence and placement for the paratroopers. The request was a dramatic one – as can be read in the report of 27 January: 'they got the Bishop to urge us to give in. When we responded that it is the property of the Holy See they required us to telephone the Holy See and give them an answer by ten o'clock the following day, the 28th, or else they would requisition all the other buildings on via San Francesco, very near the Basilica. However, we did not give in this time. To make the story short,' Fr. Mansi continues, 'let it suffice to say here that approximately fifteen times they asked for the use of the Theological College, sometimes for military use, other times for housing evacuees. We are certain that our refusal made an effective contribution to preventing the militarization of Assisi and eliminating obstacles, which would have been insur-

---

[29] The text of Fortini's letter appeared in BOLLETINO DELLA SOCIETÀ INTERNAZIONALE DI STUDI FRANCESCANI, 1946, fasc. XIV-XV-XVI, pp. 62-64; in Fortini, op cit, pp. 216-218; in Atta1, op cit., pp. 15-16.

[30] Cf. *Chronicle of the Sacro Convento.*

mountable at a later date, to naming Assisi a hospital city and thus to the salvation of the city and the evacuees.'[31]

Thus we have the point of view of the Custos at that time. Today, many years later, we feel that Fr. Mansi was right in denying the use of the Theological College for military purposes, but we fail to see his motives in denying the use of that structure for housing evacuees.

However, the praiseworthy work of the Conventuals was continuing on another front – the application for the salvation of Assisi. On 5 February, in fact, the Custos presented the following:

A new, more thorough statement to the Holy See concerning the protection of Assisi. In this new document the Holy See was informed of other buildings in Assisi which the Germans had requisitioned for military purposes and of their violent attempt on 27 January to occupy our Theological College, despite its status of exemption from requisition. There is talk of requisitioning the Umbrian Regional Seminary. Thus we can see that requisition of civilian buildings will be followed by requisition of religious ones, but even if this does not happen, the presence of operational troops quartered in civilian buildings in Assisi would constitute a grave threat to the religious buildings, sanctuaries and Franciscan monuments of the Seraphic City. The statement ended with a request that the Holy See hasten recognition of Assisi as a hospital city, observing the three points which follow:

1. That the resolve be retained by which it was agreed not to requisition buildings which are the property of the Holy See and not to militarize the whole city of Assisi, due to its mystical, spiritual, historical and artistic nature.

2. That if, because of a need to increase the number of hospitals, the Holy See would decide to allow use of the reli-

---

[31] Mansi, p. 10.

gious buildings it owns, the occupants would commit themselves to using the buildings as hospitals only, not transforming them into military housing and promising to return them immediately if they are no longer used as hospitals.

3. That the military authorities who are granted the use of religious buildings for hospitals must commit themselves not to requisition civic buildings for other purposes, so that Assisi can become a city destined exclusively for use as a hospital. Indeed, it is obvious that it would be a grave error if religious buildings of Assisi were to be used as hospitals and the civil buildings as army barracks. This would make Assisi a military objective and would bring ruin down on the whole city.[32]

While the *Chronicle of the Sacro Convento* reveals that the author of the statement is the Custos, Fr. Mansi, in reality the long petition bears the signature of the General Minister, Fr. Bede Hess,[33] who, after first mentioning his previous appeal of 4 December 1943 and recalling that the Mayor had appealed to the Government of the Republic of Italy, makes his own the ideas which had obviously been suggested to him by Fr. Mansi.

At a certain point in the statement Fr. Hess recalls that the head of the Province of Perugia, in a recent conversation with the Bishop of Assisi, Giuseppe Placido Nicolini:

offered his own proposal, saying that if Assisi does not want to have military garrisons or operational troops, it would have to increase the number of German hospitals in order to receive a greater number of the sick and wounded. 'Therefore he proposed,' this according to Fr. Bede in his statement, 'the opening of a third German hospital, and would present a formal request within a few days time. The place designated for that new hospital is the Theological Missionary College of the Friars Minor Conventual, which is the property of the Holy

---

[32] *Chronicle of the Sacro Convento.*
[33] See the document in Attal, pp. 17-21.

See...'The Bishop of Assisi, for his part,' as Fr. Bede continues to write, 'since he is the Delegate for the Sacred Congregation for Seminaries and Universities for the Regional Seminary of Umbria located in Assisi, said that he is willing to cede
the Regional Seminary for another hospital after Easter, unless
he receives orders to the contrary from his superiors.'

However, at this point we should make an observation. The
head of the Province, Dr. Rocchi, was correct. In order to save
Assisi from the German troops, it would be necessary to open
a third hospital (the first two were, the reader may recall, the
Institute for the Blind and the National Home for Orphans
of Teachers). And the Bishop had understood this. He was
willing to grant the use of the Regional Seminary for this purpose, something which he would eventually do without even
consulting the Vatican, the legal owner of the buildings, and
thus incurring the dissatisfaction of Cardinal Pizzardo.[34]
However, from Fr. Hess' statement we see that the Conventuals had not understood this:

It can be seen that the two large German military hospitals already existing in Assisi, capable of housing almost 2,000
wounded, would have fulfilled the duty of the Seraphic City
to contribute to the needs of the war and are already enough
to obtain Assisi's classification as a hospital city.

At this point we would do well to insert into the intricate
and convulsive tangle of events in that period the figure of the
physician, Colonel Valentin Müller, Commander of the German Armed Forces, to assume the direction of the German
hospitals in the city from the beginning of February 1944.[35]

---

[34] This has been confirmed by Don Aldo Brunacci, who at that time was
in the Vatican, having undergone an investigation on charges of suspected anti-
Fascism by Dr. Rocchi, head of the Province.

[35] Cf. Attal, p. 21.

However, we know that Müller was already present in the city on 5 December 1943, when a concert of spiritual music was held in the *Sala Gotica* of the Sacro Convento, directed by Fr. Domenico Stella, with the collaboration of the musical cappella of the Basilica.

On that occasion the Bishop of Assisi was seated next to Müller. The singer was an evacuee, the soprano Susanna Dango. Accompanying her on the piano was another evacuee, a man from Palermo, who had a surname that was rather risky for those times, Maestro Franco Ferrara.[36]

From that moment on, Müller's presence in Assisi would be a decisive contribution to the rapid conclusion of the plan to save the city.

His frequent meetings with the Custos of St. Francis' Basilica, (Catholic that he was, he attended daily Mass and Communion) convinced him that if Assisi was to be declared a hospital city, it would be necessary to evacuate all the German soldiers still located there.

All the other authorities of the city prodded him in this as well. First of all, Bishop Nicolini, who did so every time he invited him to dinner in the Bishop's residence or was at his side for various religious or civic celebrations in the city. And Müller did manage to convince the German authorities to remove the German military police from the Hotel Giotto and the aviators from the Hotel Subasio.[37]

---

[36] *Chronicle of the Sacro Convento*. Both Dango and Ferrara would hold another concert in Assisi, this one at the Theological College on 12 March 1944. Exactly one month after the first concert, on 6 January 1944, Colonel Müller dined with the Bishop, who was celebrating his birthday (information furnished by Fr. Otello Migliosi, former chancellor of the diocese).

[37] Attal, p. 21.

ASSISI: A HOSPITAL CITY[1]

From that time on Assisi was truly a hospital city and nothing else, and Colonel Valentin Müller was not only director of the hospitals but also military commander of the Piazza.

In the interim, Fr. Mansi's tireless work continued. Colonel Müller had told him: "You continue your work, and I'll do what I can on my part."[2]

In March 1944, for example, when the Custos of the Sacro Convento went to Padua to meet the new Director of Fine Arts for the Ministry of National Education, Prof. Carlo Anti, concerning the protection of Assisi and its artistic treasures, he asked the Minister to take the necessary steps in the Italian government to have Assisi declared a hospital city.[3]

Fortini had earlier made a similar request to Minister Biggini.[4]

At the same time the ceaseless but subtle work of the Vatican continued, and on 24 April 1944 the Secretariat of State informed the Sacro Convento that the request to have Assisi declared a hospital city was proceeding and it seemed that the desired results would be obtained before long.[5] On 24 April 1944 the Vatican Secretary of State, Cardinal Luigi Maglione, informed the General Minister that he had received and stud-

---

[1] Santucci, pp. 70-79, *Assisi "Città Ospedaliera."* Used with permission. English translation by Nancy Celaschi OSF.

[2] Ibid.

[3] Ibid. and the *Chronicle of the Sacro Convento.*

[4] Cf. Attal, p. 22.

[5] Cf. Mansi, p. 11.

ied his statement of 5 February and all the parties at war were also examining the situation. On 28 April the General Minister communicated this to the Custos, once again expressing the wish that this recognition would be granted soon.[6] This was the last letter that arrived in Assisi before the Anglo-American occupation of the city.[7]

Also concerned with the absolute demilitarization of the city was the commissioner, Mr. Checconi, who on 25 April 1944 sent a private communiqué to the German Commander of the Piazza, Colonel Müller, noting the following:

> Enclosed is a statement from the Abbess of the Monastery of St. Clare in which she complains that the German military has stored some 120 drums of petroleum near the sanctuary and many military vehicles park under the arches of the Basilica and the adjacent piazza.
>
> I must take this occasion to point out the danger caused by the presence of mobile radio transmitters in various parts of the city.
>
> I must also point out that the custodian of the medieval Rocca has informed me that in recent days German troops, despite the fact that they have seen the notice installed by Gen. Kesserling (sic) declaring the fortress a national monument under the protection of the German command, have installed a telephone line from the large tower to the small tower of the fortress itself. This certainly gives the impression that the monument may also be utilized by the German armed forces.
>
> I have taken the liberty of pointing out these things because I know of your concern for the patients in these military hospitals and I think that their interest coincides with that of the religious and artistic heritage of this city, which is today predominantly a hospital city.[8]

---

[6] Cf. *Chronicle of the Sacro Convento*.

[7] Cf. Attal, p. 23.

[8] Personal archives of Bruno Calzolari. The placement of Division n.56068, which the German Armed Forces positioned at the Giotto Hotel on 19 April

Dr. Valentin Müller in Eichstätt (ca. 1950)

Fr. Mansi could still not rest easy, and on 9 May he received permission from the German military command in Italy to go to Florence "to confer with the Ministry of Culture concerning questions about Assisi."[9] Under the date of Saturday, 17 May, we read in the *Chronicle of the Sacro Convento*:

> In Florence the Custos conferred with the Colonel and with Dr. Langsdorff, German Head of Office for the Care of Art in Italy. Present for the discussions were the Director of the Institute for the History of German Art and the Superintendent of the Galleries of Florence, Dr. Giovanni Poggi. The Custos informed the Colonel of the exemption of the Basilica from any search or requisition since it is the property of the Holy See, recognized as such by the German Supreme Command. The Custos also asked the Colonel to intervene with the proper German authorities to hasten recognition of Assisi as a 'hospital city,' and that precise indications concerning this be given to Colonel Müller, German Commander of the hospitals of Assisi. This was not only in relation to Assisi's historic importance but also because of the new depository of the works of art that had been created there. The German Colonel assured the Custos that the very next day he would send the Supreme Command of the German Forces in Italy a report totally in favor of his request.[10]

Besides the Custos and Prof. Alexander Langsdorff, the meeting was attended by Dr. Heinrich Heydenreich, Director of the German Institute of the History of Art in Florence and director of the department for the care of art in Tuscany and Umbria.[11] At the same time Colonel Müller was doing his part, designating other buildings of the city for use as mili-

---

1944 did not constitute a provocation for the Allies, perhaps because it passed unobserved. Ibid.

[9] *Chronicle of the Sacro Convento.*

[10] Ibid.

[11] Cf. Attal, p. 23.

tary hospitals. Besides the Locatelli Palace, the Seraphic Institute for the Deaf, Dumb and Blind, the National Home for Orphans of Teachers (later the Oasis of the Sacred Heart[12]) and the Umbrian Regional Seminary would house wounded German soldiers.[13] On 5 June the superiors of the Sacro Convento decided to give Colonel Müller the use of the upper floor of the Theological College to establish a hospital section there.[14] By this time things were ready to have Assisi declared a "hospital city." In fact, all the conditions had been met. The Holy See had been very much involved in advancing this with the Allied governments. The German command was directly interested in such recognition to guarantee the safety of the thousands of wounded being treated in the hospitals of Assisi. Even the Italian government (although obviously it did not carry much weight in any decision-making on the matter) had been asked several times for such recognition. Now the city was truly a hospital city, and nothing else.

And of course, there was the art to safeguard, and everyone was aware of this – the Germans, the Vatican, the Anglo-Americans (we need only recall the art collection of the famous American art critic, F.M. Perkins, had been brought to the Sacro Convento).[15]

In the second half of May the news had spread. The radio had announced that Assisi had been proclaimed an "open city." However, as we shall see, that was not exactly true.[16]

---

[12] Ibid., p. 24.

[13] Cf. A. Brunacci, *L'opera di assistenza del clero e del vescovo di Assisi dopo l'8 settembre 1943 in Cattolici e fascisti in Umbria (1922-1945)*, A. Monticone, ed. Bologna, Il Mulino, 1978, p. 453.

[14] Cf. Mansi, p. 11.

[15] In this regard see the chapter dedicated to the protection of cultural goods. Perkins would later donate a collection of 57 paintings to the Sacro Convento.

[16] Cf. Attal, p. 24.

Regardless of the fact of whether or not that rumor was true, on 19 May the British representative to the Holy See gave the assurance that for his government's part, "although not disposed to proceed with the above-mentioned recognition, it would assume precaution for the safety of the hospitals and artistic treasures of the Seraphic City and that very strict instructions to that effect had been given to the commanders of the Allied air forces."[17]

On 30 May in a letter numbered b. 7985/S, Bishop Giovanni Battista Montini of the Vatican Secretariat of State, wrote to Fr. Bede Hess, asking him to communicate this to the Custos of the Sacro Convento. However, because of the difficulties of that period, the letter never reached Assisi.[74] In fact, there is no trace of it in the archives of the Sacro Convento. Thus the Vatican's work had been crowned with success. In just a little while the efforts on the other front – the German front – would also yield their desired effect.

On 31 May, in fact, the German Ambassador to the Holy See, "in reply to the notes numbered 78066/S of 24 April and 2549/44 of 5 May concerning the city of Assisi," communicated: "the 'Generalissimo'[19] of the German Forces in Italy has consented to Assisi being declared a 'hospital city.' According to his declaration, at present there is nothing in Assisi except field hospitals and medical units. The same Generalissimo has prohibited the occupation of the city of Assisi by other troops or commands of the *Wehrmacht*."[20]

The greatly desired news, however, communicated by the Secretariat of State, reached Assisi only on 21 June, after the city's liberation, in a letter from Cardinal Maglione addressed

---

[17] Ibid. and Fortini, p. 219.

[18] Cf. Attal, p. 24.

[19] An obvious reference to Kesselring.

[20] Cf. Attal, p. 24 and Fortini, p. 219.

to Fr. Bede Hess.[21] However, some people in Assisi must have been aware of this matter. On 31 May Colonel Müller went with four officers to give verbal communication of this news to Bishop Nicolini.[22] It was during that meeting that Colonel Müller asked Bishop Nicolini, the Holy See's delegate for the Umbrian Regional Seminary, for the use of that large complex just below Assisi on the old road to the Porziuncola.

Although the Bishop knew he should have first asked the Holy See, the owner of the complex, for such permission, he nonetheless told the German Colonel that he could certainly house wounded German soldiers in the seminary. As we have noted before, when news of that concession reached the Vatican, it provoked the wrath of Cardinal Giuseppe Pizzardo, Prefect of the Sacred Congregation for Seminaries.

The Bishop's decision was critical for Assisi's safety. If, in fact, the regional seminary had not been conceded for the care of the wounded, it would have certainly been requisitioned by the SS or other German troops. That would have inevitably provoked a reaction from the Allies, and thus the bombing of the area immediately adjacent to the city. Therefore, in the afternoon of 3 June 1944, the Umbrian Regional Seminary received its first wounded German soldiers.[23]

Another decisive action of the Bishop to remove the threat of Allied bombing was that "several times he used" all his influence to "prevent the occupation of the house of Mr. Tibetio Gualdi by the German military forces,"[24] since that villa was situated right at Assisi's gates, on the road to Santa Maria degli Angeli.

---

[21] Cf. Attal, p. 24.

[22] Cf. Brunacci, p. 453.

[23] Cf. V. Falcinelli, Torgiano, I. Lavoro – Religione – Folclore, S. Maria degli Angeli, Tip. Porziuncola 1977, p. 432.

[24] AVA, Bishop Nicolini fund, a. 1944, b. Periodico bellico. Actually, that villa was supposed to be officially "used for the lodging of German troops," as can be read in an undated dispatch sent from Munich (Bruno Calzolari archives).

Valentin Müller as a student in Würzburg

That is precisely how things developed. For some time a German division had been lodged there, but they were officially used for medical work, taking care of the treatment of the German wounded. In reality, however, more than once the Allied airplanes heading for the airfield of Sant'Egidio were greeted by antiaircraft fire from Villa Gualdi.

This fact was noted especially by Mr. Gualdi, who had been forced to let the Germans use his villa. He himself lived across the street in another house he owned. And so, as the gentleman himself later recounted the events, he went to the Bishop's residence and reported this to Bishop Nicolini. The Bishop called Colonel Müller, who saw to it that the German division was immediately removed from Villa Gualdi, and he placed another small hospital there.

Several days before his meeting with Bishop Nicolini, Colonel Müller went to Foligno for a meeting with Marshall Kesselring, who had established his headquarters there.[25]

On that occasion Kesselring had informed him that things were going well for Assisi's recognition as a hospital city. But Müller expressed his concern that the retreating German troops might occupy the city. Kesselring then informed him that he would issue a special order forbidding German military troops from entering Assisi.[26]

Müller's generous and self-sacrificing work, however, was not yet finished. When, in fact, the first retreating German troops arrived on the plain below Assisi, the Colonel placed guards around the clock at all the gates of the city, using his own hospital personnel, to prevent the German troops from entering the city.[27]

Müller also had a barricade placed at Santa Maria degli Angeli, also near Santa Maria delle Grazie, to make the last

---

[25] Cf. A. Bowl, *Order of the Day*, London, Leo Cooper, 1974, p. 98.
[26] Ibid.
[27] Ibid.

retreating German troops understand that they were not to go up to Assisi.[28] Indeed, Müller knew that Assisi's salvation was in the city remaining completely demilitarized until the front had completely passed it by.

As the Anglo-American troops drew nearer, during the second week of June, Müller received orders to evacuate the 2,000 German wounded and the hospital personnel from Assisi. He took personal command of the whole operation to make sure that no harm was done to anything that was being abandoned – buildings, furnishings, equipment.

The convoy of the wounded left the city on the morning of 15 June and Müller entrusted it to the command of his assistant. He wanted to remain in Assisi until the very last moment.

The Allies were already on the plain between Foligno and Rivotorto. The German rear guard arrived that very same day at Santa Maria degli Angeli. There was a risk that those German soldiers might come up to Assisi to set up positions. Müller alone was capable of averting that danger. It is true that there were very exact promises not to do that, made by Kesselring the previous month, but there was still a danger. Moreover, the rear guard was a battalion of SS troops, known for their atrocities and autonomy. If they had decided to go to Assisi it would be the end of all the diplomatic efforts which had been going on for ten months. In fact, the presence of SS troops in Assisi would have inevitably provoked an Allied attack upon the city.

Therefore, as night fell on 15 June, Müller positioned himself outside the main gate of Assisi. From the valley he heard the sounds of demolition and could see the striking images of buildings set afire by the angry SS troops.

The next day some of the SS troops came up to Assisi. Müller and they began a heated debate, but the verbal exchange did

---

[28] Information furnished by Mr. Carmelo Piazza, a resident of Santa Maria degli Angeli.

not last long. It was long enough, however, for him to convince the German rear guard to abandon the city. Assisi was safe!

Shortly after midnight on 16 June Colonel Müller and his division set out on the road leading north.[29]

---

[29] Cf. Bowl, pp. 99-100.

THE LIBERATION[1]

Before retreating the Germans mined and exploded the villa at Colle dei Benzi near Viole, the Costanzi mill at Santa Maria degli Angeli, also the bridge over the Chiascio at Petrignano d'Assisi.

On the morning of 17 June the Allies, coming from Foligno on the road through Viole, entered Assisi. But they arrived in tanks and personnel carriers, thus violating the city's "hospital" status, although it should be remembered that the aforementioned status had been conferred by the unilateral decision of the Germans.

Concerning those dramatic last hours, so decisive for Assisi's safety, we have these brief notes taken from the *Chronicle of the Sacro Convento*:[2]

16. Friday: During the night the English began bombardments in the valley, and they drew closer. The Assisians and all the others ran to the tomb of the Saint and, along with the religious, repeatedly recited the rosary and other prayers. Under these dreadful circumstances the tomb and the lower Basilica were turned into a public dormitory, as it were.

17 June: Around 9:30 this morning the Anglo-American troops entered Assisi by means of the Porta Nova and Porta Santa Chiara, passed through the city, came through the lower piazza and stopped on the level area where they opened fire.

---

[1] Santucci, pp. 79-92. *La Liberazione*. Used with permission. English translation by Nancy Celaschi OSF.

[2] Archives of the Sacro Convento, ms.

From the surrounding hillsides the Germans returned their fire, hitting a few houses and a grenade also struck the bastion of Sixtus IV. There was no significant damage, however. All of Assisi was draped with banners and the bells sounded. Our Basilica kept out of the manifestations because this was the most delicate time for its safety.

In the afternoon the German artillery barrage continued, and the Anglo-American forces returned their fire. The people sought refuge in the Basilica.[3]

Of interest also are these notes from the *Chronicle of the Protoconvent* at Rivotorto concerning the day before the liberation:

16 June: At about five o'clock in the evening the bells were tolling for the funeral of the deceased Carmela Ronca and, as is our custom, the bell tolling was prolonged. Suddenly there was automatic weapons fire against the door of the convent and the community was alarmed. Father Leo, who was talking with some men against the wall of the first arcade of the cloister, was not immediately aware of the danger, but then as the gunfire was repeated, he and the men took refuge in the storage area where wood is kept, an area whose door opens onto the main highway. From there he called to Fr. Alessandro who was in his room on the upper floor, so that from his window overlooking the main door he could call down to the soldiers and explain the situation to them. However, without any warning the scene changed. Fr. Leo, followed by the others, left his refuge. Upon seeing this, Fr. Alessandro climbed up into the tower, removed the ladder, and lay down flat in a hidden corner of the roof to wait and see what happened. About an hour passed until he heard Fr. Leo calling him from one of the windows in the bell tower. Fr. Leo was pale and shaking. Fr. Alessandro realized that something terrible had happened to him. There was no time

---

[3] Ibid.

to waste on explanations. Rather, they must immediately remove the Papal flag that was flying above the church. This could only be done by means of a ladder within the bell tower. What had happened?

The Germans had tried unsuccessfully to break down the main door, so they began working on the side door, and they had guessed correctly. However, the refugees had succeeded in making their way into the convent by the main stairway. So Fr. Leo decided to go to the soldiers and explain. Therefore, they went down the internal stairway and went through the church and there they met the soldiers. A voice shouted out to them that they were being accused of treason because of the tolling of the bells, the flag flying over the church and the closed doors. No explanations were accepted. They are "traitors" and must pay the price. They forced them to line up and aimed their rifles at them. But Fr. Leo was not about to die without trying to explain their innocence, and then explained, as best he could, their three imagined "crimes." He begged and pleaded with them, but it was all in vain. However, only one soldier was moved by the priest's pleas, and succeeded in persuading the others of their innocence. The adventure closed with a few kicks and the categorical command to remove the flag immediately. Besides Fr. Leo, the condemned included parishioners Giuseppe Salucci, Artemio Capitini and Enzo Gubbiotti. By seven o'clock everything was peaceful.

There were no more tanks or personnel carriers. No more soldiers. Some explosions could be heard in the area of Santa Maria degli Angeli and nothing more. This was a sure sign that we were in territory that for now was free and that in a short time we would be the prey of the advancing troops.

In the darkness of the night we could see clearly the fires coming from Montecatini and the Costanzi mill and an immense German tank which had been set afire by the retreating troops some 200 meters away from the church. Perhaps it was these fires that caused the Allies to turn their cannons on us, because at eleven o'clock a terrible bombardment began. It lasted for two hours. The two priests and two men from the parish (young Umberto Lena and Carmelo Giannuzzi had been sent to Assisi to the Theological College) did not take this seriously, since they thought they were explosions coming from munitions in the burning tank. Therefore, throughout the worst of the explosions, as the windows were shattered and stones and plaster fell, they were rather calm, protected by the strong walls on the ground floor.

When morning came they saw the widespread damage and realized how great a danger they had been in. All the windows of the church and convent were shattered. The window frames, door frames and doors were reduced to rubble. A main wall of the house had been penetrated by a howitzer shell, which had landed in the roomful of beds used by the young students, which was nothing but a mass of twisted iron. Everywhere they looked there were marks on the ceiling, chunks taken out of the walls, and holes in the eaves.[4]

Late in the morning of 17 June some cannon shells fired by the retreating German troops (who, it was said, were firing from Colcaprile and the hills of San Fortunato because they heard the bells in Assisi tolling in celebration and they saw the Italian flag flying above the Hotel Savoia) struck the Abbey of San Pietro and the monastery of the French Collettine nuns.[5] Some shells even grazed the dome of Santa Maria degli Angeli.

At the Porta San Giacomo two people were killed[6] and several were wounded. Several pieces of shrapnel fell near Porta San Francesco, seriously wounding a young man from Assisi who was returning to Perugia, where he worked as a fire fighter and a 15 year old boy, who died a short time later.[7]

---

[4] Archives of the Protoconvento at Rivotorto.

[5] Archives of the monastery of the Sisters of St. Colette, ms.

[6] Roberto Raggi, a native of Eboli in the province of Salerno, who was a refugee in Assisi, and Francesco Chiarini, of San Giacomo (cf. Notiziario Assisano, 18 June 1994, p. 1).

[7] The fireman was Leonello Costantini, who was taken to the hospital where, after a long agony and terrible suffering – and in part due to a lack of

Bas relief on the tomb of Bishop Nicolini

Concerning the events of those two eventful days, we read in the *Chronicles of the Convent* of the Capuchins in Assisi:

16 June: This evening was infernal. It seemed as if the end of the world had come. Fire was consuming everything. The retreating Germans gave vent to their anger, setting fire to everything and ruining even more than they could. The whole plain around Assisi was alight with the dancing of the flames. Mills, silos, body shops, all types of storage areas were set afire. Bridges, stations and villas were blown apart. Large numbers of animals had been taken from their owners and carried off....

17 June: With the retreat of the Germans and all the devastation which they willingly and knowingly inflicted upon

---

medicine – he died on 2 July, leaving a wife and three young children. He was 35 years old. The boy was Giuseppe Piantoni, known to all as "Peppino." Some of the shells hit the road where the Allied troops were passing. In that barrage a British soldier was also killed, and was given a hasty burial alongside the road. (Information furnished by Bruno Calzolari).

us poor Italians whom they called traitors, this morning at 9:30 the English entered the piazza of the city on top of a few armored cars. They were greeted by the festive tolling of bells and an immense crowd of people. The city was immediately arrayed in British and American flags, and everyone strove to celebrate our new bosses, our liberators. After discourses by various dignitaries, the English left the city, stopping for a brief time at the Piazza San Francesco.

This great celebration was followed immediately by another fright. The Germans had taken up positions in the surrounding hills and saw the British enter the city which they had not been allowed to enter since it was a hospital city, and completely demilitarized. Therefore they began to fire upon the city.[8]

That very same day the local National Liberation Committee posted notices on all the walls of the city and the surrounding towns calling for a moral and spiritual rebirth in Italy.[9]

---

[8] Archives of the Capuchin Convent in Assisi, *Cronaca del Convento*, written by Fr. Alberto of Gubbio.

[9] Editors' note: They had survived one danger, but a new danger now arose: the establishment of armed Allied troops in the city could have provoked German air raids.

Bishop Nicolini continued his appeals to the Vatican and the Allied commanders over the next several months, so that neither armed troops nor their commanders nor any military supplies would be brought into the city.

THE TRUE STORY[1]

The book by Professor Francesco Santucci – *Assisi 1943-44 Documenti Per Una Storia* – published under the auspices of the *Accademia Properziana del Subasio* in 1994 on the occasion of the 50th anniversary of the city's liberation, has aroused great interest not only in Italy, but in other countries as well. This is to be expected, given the city's renown throughout the world and the truly heroic role its citizens played in 1943-1944 on behalf of several thousand refugees – including several hundred Jews as well as political refugees – all of whom came to the city of St. Francis confident of finding safety there.

At the end of the German occupation, 17 June 1944, all the refugees were able to return to their own homes, including many Jews, each of whom expressed gratitude to the Bishop of Assisi. Among the testimonials that Santucci includes in his appendix, page 136, is one by Prof. Emilio Viterbi, a scientist and dean at the University of Padua, who, together with his wife and two daughters, were lovingly welcomed and helped in Assisi.

On 15 May 1944, when the notorious Prefect Rocchi of Perugia sent police to arrest me, Emilio Viterbi and his wife were waiting for me in my office on Via San Francesco, because they no longer felt safe in their home and were in search of some other place of refuge. Fortunately the soldiers

[1] By Don Aldo Brunacci. Previously published in *The Strategy That Saved Assisi*, Editrice Minerva Assisi 2000, pp. 7-13, this article was reworked for this edition. Used with permission.

were not aware of their presence, because I closed the door behind me as I was led away.

In their confusion they knew to whom they could appeal. Prof. Viterbi writes:

> During the last period of the occupation the episcopal palace of Bishop Nicolini had become an asylum for a great number of refugees and persons who were being persecuted. Nonetheless, when I went to him to ask if, in the case of extreme difficulty, he could house me and my family, with great simplicity and a gentle smile, he said: 'There is no room left except my bedroom and my office. However, I can sleep in my office. The bedroom is yours.' This is what this distinguished prelate of Assisi was like.

Professor Santucci is the person with the best knowledge of Assisi's history today, for which reason he has been entrusted with the task of caring for the valuable archives of the Cathedral and Chancery. He has painstakingly examined all the documents of the many archives in the city and has succeeded in giving us a thorough view of this historical period, showing how much was being done for the liberation of Assisi.

Nor could I fail to add my observations, since at that time I was Bishop Nicolini's only collaborator and the secretary of the diocesan hospitality center at the Bishop's residence. To this center came refugees from cities that had been bombarded, Jews, and even many of Assisi's young people who spent their nights in the areas near the Bishop's house to avoid the German soldiers' nighttime military exercises.

Even before Prof. Santucci, Francesco Salvatore Attal, a Jew who converted to Catholicism, published an article entitled *Assisi Città Santa Come Fu Salvata dagli Orrori della Guerra* (*Assisi: The Holy City and How It Was Preserved from the Horrors of War*)[2].

---

[2] MISCELLANEA FRANCESCANA, periodical of the theological faculty of the Conventual Friars in Rome (volume 48, 1948, fasc. I, p. 132).

Don Aldo Brunacci

The author reports primarily on the letter-writing campaign between the religious and civil authorities, especially the Custos of the Sacro Convento, to protect the Basilica of St. Francis. However, in my opinion, he was not well-informed about the whole complex period under consideration.

Santucci also calls one of his chapters "Protecting the Cultural Resources." He shows that from January 1943 onwards, this was of great concern to the Superintendent of Medieval and Modern Art, Mr. Achille Bertini Calosso. In this regard Santucci mentions appeals to the warring parties made by the Minister of the Friars Minor Conventual, Fr. Bede Hess, an American citizen; by the Custos of the Sacro Convento, Fr Bonaventura Manzi; by the Bishop of Assisi, Placido Nicolini; and by the former Mayor of Assisi, Arnaldo Fortini, who also appealed to Mussolini – leader of the Republic of Salò by that time and having no real authority.

Santucci recounted this in order to be historically accurate, but in the end – and I, an eyewitness of what happened in Assisi at that time, could not be more in agreement with him – he had to state: "The city owed its salvation primarily to the fact that it had been proclaimed a hospital city." Thus it was not spared bombardment solely because of the invaluable artistic treasures it housed.

If that had been the real reason Assisi was saved, how could we explain the fact that the Abbey of Montecassino – of no less importance culturally and spiritually than the city of St. Francis – was destroyed. We must conclude that the two people most responsible for saving Assisi were Bishop Giuseppe Placido Nicolini, and Colonel Valentin Müller – a German officer – yes, an officer of Hitler's army.

Who was Valentin Müller? He was a medical officer, born in 1891 and died in 1951. In February 1944 this medical doctor was put in charge of the German hospitals in the city by the commanders of the German armed forces. The Colonel was a very religious man who attended daily mass and communion at the tomb of St. Francis.

With the Bishop's help, he realized that the only way to save the city would be to increase the number of hospitals in it so that it could be proclaimed a "hospital city." The Bishop worked closely with him in this matter. He was sure that this was the only way they could save the city of St. Francis, for whom Müller, as a Catholic, had a great love.

The front drew ever nearer and the number of the wounded grew. On 31 May – as I was told by the parish priest, Don Lamberto Petrucci – Colonel Müller and four other officers went to San Vitale where the Bishop was celebrating a parish feast. The Colonel asked the Bishop to grant him the use of the Pontifical Seminary of Umbria as a military hospital. The Bishop knew quite well that the seminary was the property of the Holy See, but because of the city's more compelling interest, he did not hesitate to grant the Colonel's request. As of that date, 31 May, the following buildings were used as hospitals:

- the Locatelli Palace (now Casa Papa Giovanni);
- the Seraphic Institute for the Blind and Deaf;
- the National Home for Orphans of Teachers;
- the Oasis of the Sacred Heart;
- the Umbrian Regional Seminary.

On 5 June, following repeated requests, the friars of the Sacro Convento also decided to allow Colonel Müller to use the top floor of their Theological College as well. The warring parties recognized Assisi as a hospital city and for this reason it was respected.

Let me repeat that the two people most responsible for Assisi's safety were Bishop Nicolini and Colonel Müller. Müller's role was gratefully acknowledged by Assisi when it dedicated a street in his memory and installed a memorial plaque on Viale Vittorio Emanuele II, directly across from the Seraphic Institute, which was the first German military hospital in Assisi. Colonel Müller returned to Assisi during the Holy Year 1950, and was warmly welcomed by the entire city which had never forgotten him. When he left, he promised to return again. Several months later, however, he became ill and died soon after in his hometown.

In 1982, the eighth centenary of the birth of St. Francis, a delegation from Assisi went to Eichstätt to place olive branches from the hillsides of Assisi on Colonel Müller's grave. I had the honor of presiding at the prayers by his tomb and we were all moved to see carved on his tombstone the outline of the Basilica of St. Francis.

Bishop Nicolini's tomb is in the Chapel of the Pietà (to the left of the main altar) in the Cathedral of San Rufino. He died in the city of Trent, but the people of Assisi wanted him to return to the Church where he so frequently proclaimed the Gospel of peace. A bas-relief by Enrico Manfrini shows the Bishop with his mantle spread wide and children taking refuge under it[3]. He was father of all the people during his episcopate in Assisi. However, in 1943/44 he was father as well of all those who took refuge in our city.

Before concluding this introduction, I feel it is my duty to point out that for the first time ever Prof. Santucci published a hand-written document of Bishop Nicolini: "The Story of the Medical Supplies."[4] This refers to a great quantity of medicine and medical equipment that Colonel Müller, after the retreat of German troops, left behind in the city at great risk to himself. Unfortunately, a large part of this material was lost.

What Santucci is referring to is a direct communiqué from the chancery which I personally drafted at the time, following the Bishop's very clear instructions. This document also casts suspicion on the hero of the book, *Assisi Underground*,

---

[3] See p. 57.
[4] See p. 102.

in which he was presented as Bishop Nicolini's collaborator. This lie was accepted most of all in America, to the point that in the Holocaust Memorial Museum in Washington, D.C., in the entry under the name of Nicolini, we find Father Rufino Nicacci mentioned as his collaborator. No greater offense could have been given to a person like Bishop Placido Nicolini, who at great risk, saved so many Jews in Assisi.

Santucci's book does not go into the debate but simply presents the documentary evidence and renders justice against a book that has sold many copies as well as being made into a film.

In conclusion, I would like to join the President of the *Accademia Properziana del Subasio*, Prof. Giuseppe Catanzaro, in stating that the publication of such precious and unique documents allows us to have precise knowledge of so many events and episodes of human solidarity. It will be evident to all how, in a period of passion and opposing views, a few citizens, some known to us and others forgotten, had overcome, even at great risk to their own persons, the divisions between ideologies and saw in each person a brother or sister whom they must save.

THE UNSUNG HERO: BISHOP NICOLINI[1]

By way of several different publications I have tried to satisfy people's legitimate desire to know the truth about what was described by Alessandro Ramati in his book, *Assisi Clandestina* which was first published in Italian in 1982 by Porziuncola Press and was made into a film. (The English translation of the book was published under the title: *The Assisi Underground*.) It is truly a wonderful work of fiction, but pure fiction because it distorts the historical truth of a glorious period of Assisi's history, in which the main character of Ramati's book and film did not really play a leading role. I can state unequivocally that the true unsung hero of the period under discussion was Bishop Giuseppe Placido Nicolini, Bishop of Assisi at that time. I served as his sole comrade in this work, because the very nature of it required that he not take many into his confidence. On 5 January 1947, in an article entitled *The Heart of the Bishop During the War*, I wrote the following:

> Who is capable of writing the chronicle of such heroism, of such charity? Who could possibly describe the work of our pastor in this our Assisi which, in fulfillment of St. Francis' prophecy, has never before been the refuge, the material and spiritual salvation of so many of the faithful as it was during this war? After the well-known events of July 1943 the Bishop's house became the single center of assistance for the

---

[1] By Don Aldo Brunacci. Previously published in *The Strategy That Saved Assisi,* Editrice Minerva Assisi 2000, pp. 7-13, this article was reworked for this edition. Used with permission.

many people who poured into the city from other cities under bombardment or from the front, which daily grew closer. That period saw the establishment of the Committee for Assistance, presided over by the Bishop, who continued his wide-reaching charitable activity until the end of the war. This committee, made up of diligent people, saw to the settlement of an immigrant population that at times equaled the population of the city. It created a center for the collection of essential items, especially of clothing, and a workshop was even established in the Bishop's residence.

Those who were fleeing persecution most of all found in Bishop Nicolini a shepherd with a Christ-like heart, and a welcome that could make them forget the hatred they were experiencing. In response to the Bishop's invitation, the convents and various religious communities took in about a hundred Jews and victims of persecution of every type. All this required a clandestine activity and a rather complex organization, which only a magnanimous person like Bishop Nicolini could have created.

The Bishop's kindness reached everywhere. Several times people who had just arrived and were waiting to be taken in somewhere else, or who were in imminent danger, were given refuge and a bed in the only room the Bishop had left. This great charitable activity never failed, despite the dangers, risks and threats of those who were watching over the work performed by the Bishop and myself. I will never forget how insistent those threats were, yet how determined the Bishop remained. He would not let anyone intimidate him from performing what he as pastor was required to do.

I recall very well the strength Bishop Nicolini showed in the face of the repeated alarms of the 'big shots' who felt it was their duty to suggest prudence and moderation. There are times in everyone's life in which it is easy to confuse prudence with a calm life. There are times when heroism is required. Bishop Nicolini took the path of heroism.

It is for this reason that when I was planning a pilgrimage to Jerusalem in December of 1977 and was invited to receive

Jerusalem, 11 December 1977: the Bishop of Assisi Dino Tomassini (right) and Don Aldo Brunacci (left) with a group of Jews saved in Assisi during the war, receive the Medal of the Righteous Gentiles from the State of Israel the medal and honors which the government of Israel reserves to those who worked to save Jews during World War II, I said that I was unable to accept this recognition unless it was first awarded to the person who was the true moving force behind this action. They replied that Bishop Nicolini had passed away. But I replied that the current Bishop of Assisi, as his successor, could receive the honor in his name.

The, ceremony took place on 11 December 1977, and was covered by the Israeli media. In a two-column article, the Jerusalem Post wrote: "The late Bishop of Assisi, Italy, who used the city's convents and monasteries to hide a hundred Jews during World War II, and his main collaborator, now Prior of the Cathedral of San Rufino in Assisi, will be honored in a ceremony at Yad Vashem in the Avenue of the Just. Representing the late Bishop will be his successor, Bishop." Dino Tomassini, who is in Israel conducting a pilgrimage.

Following the ceremony for the planting of a tree with a marker written in Hebrew and Italian, bearing the names of Bishop Giuseppe Placido Nicolini and Prof. Aldo Brunacci in the Park of the Just, an official reception was held in which Bishop Tomassini was given a certificate and medal in honor of Bishop Giuseppe Placido Nicolini, and I received the same. Each time that the speaker mentioned Bishop Nicolini's name, it was followed by the Biblical blessing, "may he be blessed forever."

I still have very many vivid memories of that time, and I would like to share some of them with you, dear readers. I am not always able to establish the exact date on which they occurred because prudence dictated that nothing should be written down.

One Thursday in September 1943, after the usual monthly meeting of the clergy in the diocesan seminary, the Bishop called me aside during a recess near the chapel and showed me a letter from the Vatican Secretariat of State and said to me: "We have to organize ourselves to help those who are being persecuted, especially the Jews. This is the desire of the Holy Father, Pope Pius XII. Everything must be done with the greatest secrecy and prudence. No one, not even the priests, must know anything about this."[2]

As I mentioned before, the Bishop's residence already hosted a center for aid to the refugees from areas afflicted by the war, and therefore it was not difficult to insert this new and sensitive action on behalf of the Jews into this vast organization. The Bishop's residence was spacious and had underground rooms. It was often necessary to hide, not only persons, but also the personal effects of those who were given refuge in the convents and private homes. There were precious objects, family mementos, and even objects and vestments for Jewish religious services, sacred texts – for there

---

[2] In the book, *Pio XII, il privilegio di servirlo*, by Pascalina Lehnert (Rusconi Ed. 1984), one reads the following regarding the secret, and therefore efficacious work of Pius XII on behalf of the Jews:

"I recall in horror that morning in August 1942 when the newspaper headlines reported the horrible news that the official protest of the Dutch Bishops against the inhuman persecution of the Jews had led Hitler to take revenge by arresting 40,000 Jews that very night and sending them off to the gas chambers. The morning newspapers were brought to the Holy Father's study as he was getting ready for an audience. He only read the headlines, and turned pale. When he returned from his audience, it was already one o'clock, time for lunch, and before going to the dining room the Holy Father came into the kitchen (the only place it would have been possible to burn something unobserved), with two large pieces of paper covered with writing, and said: 'I want to burn these papers. It is my protest against the terrible persecution of the Jews. It was supposed to be printed in L'OSSERVATORE ROMANO this evening. But if the letter of the Dutch Bishops cost 40,000 human lives, my protest might cost 200,000. I cannot and must not take this responsibility. Therefore, it is better not to speak out officially and continue to do in silence everything humanly possible for these people'" [pp. 148-149]. Two Dutch Jews escaped the retaliation and, after various vicissitudes, made their way to Assisi. Their name was Jacobson. I remember their inconsolable tears as they told me how the German soldiers led their two young sons, both in their twenties, away from home and they were never heard from again.

The "commission of the just" honors Bishop Nicolini on 11 December 1977

were some rabbis among the refugees – and all those items had to be kept in a place of greatest security.[3] These items were placed in recesses in the subterranean vault of the Bishop's residence and then walled over. The work was not done by workers, but by the Bishop himself who used the trowel to build the walls while I held the lantern. When a wall had to be broken into, I would wield the pick while the Bishop held the light for me. These operations were performed whenever we had to restore objects to individuals who were leaving Assisi even before the end of the war.

8 October 1943. The Jewish refugees in Assisi were celebrating their first Yom Kippur away from their homes, and for some of them, away from their homeland. I would like to quote what I wrote in an article for the *Catholic Times of London* on 19 August 1946:

> After the liberation the news about Assisi was reported with sensationalism by the foreign press For example, an English newspaper reported that the Jews in Assisi were able to have a synagogue in the crypt of the monastery founded by St. Francis. There is some truth in that article – that the Jews were absolutely free to gather for prayer in the quiet of the convents of Assisi – because it happened that, while the Sisters were intent on their prayer, under that same roof the Jews were invoking God's mercy and asking for peace and justice. On 8 December 1943 a group of various nationalities was

---

[3] Editors' note: Did Colonel Müller have any idea about this? According to his son Robert: "If he was deceived, it is because he wanted to be deceived. If he had known, he would not have done anything to stop it. As a matter of fact, the house where he established his practice in Eichstätt had been purchased from a Jewish family. He paid for it in cash, allowing them to escape immediately. My father was also the last medical doctor to make visits to the homes of Jewish patients." Maximilian Schell, who portrayed Colonel Müller in the film version of Ramati's book, obviously depicted a very different character. From all that can be deduced, if Müller had known, he would not have acted differently.

gathered in the Monastery of San Quirico to celebrate the feast of Yom Kippur. The nuns had had the wonderful idea of decorating the dining room and the tables for a feast day. When the guests sat down to table to take their first meal after the feast and looked around, they no longer felt like strangers and they understood that in the bond of love they had been welcomed as brothers and sisters. I recall what a day of intense emotion that was!

9 November 1943. It was approximately seven o'clock in the morning. I was celebrating Mass at the Laboratorio San Francesco at the ancient Church of "Muro Rupto." During the celebration I was surprised to see Mrs. Krops from Trieste and her sister, Mrs. Maionica, waiting for me. At the end of Mass, amid their anguish they were able to tell me that the elderly Mrs. Weiss from Vienna, who had been suffering from cardiac problems for a few days, had died during the night, despite the care of Mrs. Maionica's doctor son. I had gone to visit her the previous day. Now we were faced with the problem of her burial. I hurried with them to San Quirico and, after saying a brief prayer over the body, told the ladies I would take care of everything. No one at the city offices was surprised that an elderly refugee had died in Assisi. I explained that she had given me the money to buy a burial place in the cemetery in my name.

That same day, as dusk was beginning to fall, accompanied by very few people, we carried her to the cemetery. The evening was very cold. When we arrived at the cemetery we had the coffin placed, as usual, at the entrance of the chapel. I went to the custodian, Guerrino Lanfaloni, my elementary school classmate, and told him: "It is too cold to have the customary prayers here. We did everything at San Quirico. Let us take the coffin immediately into the mortuary and bury her tomorrow." On the tomb we placed an inscription naming her "Bianca Bianchi," translating her surname into its Italian equivalent. It remained like this until war's end. As we silently proceeded along the road towards the cemetery, we ran into a German patrol whose members immediately stood at attention, never knowing that the coffin they saluted contained the body of a Jewish lady. At the end of the war Mrs. Weiss' son came to visit. He had taken refuge in Brazil. I went with him to his mother's tomb, and together we made arrangements to have the stone changed. Today the tomb of Mrs. Weiss can still be found in the cemetery of Assisi, with the Star of David above this inscription: KERFA FELD CLARA, widow WEISS, born at Vienna on 15 September 1887 and died peacefully in Assisi, where she had found loving hospitality during the Nazi persecution, on 9 November 1943.

I have many memories of that time that I could share with you, some of them happy and some not so happy. However, I would also like to mention some of those who worked with me in helping our Jewish brothers and sisters, and who are no longer among the living. First in chronological order was the Conventual, Fr. Michele Todde, from the Basilica of St. Francis. It was he who sent us the first group of Jews, who were then lodged in San Quirico. The Church of St. Francis was a natural place for those who came to Assisi seeking help. Fr. Todde knew all the places in which we were hiding people, and which we continually changed, for obvious reasons: the Laboratorio San Francesco, the Convent of the German Sisters, the Cathedral and the Diocesan Seminary.

Fr. Rufino Nicacci OFM, in his role as guardian of San Damiano, often went to San Quirico. Thus he befriended the first group that was given refuge there, and he joined our clandestine organization, offering courageous assistance because of this courageous enterprise. Fr. Federico Vincenti, was parish priest of Sant' Andrea in Perugia, whose parish was another point of reference. A group of young Jews lived in the attic of his home. I also slept in this attic when I went to Perugia by bicycle on sensitive missions at dusk. In the morning I would go back to Assisi by bicycle, joining up with the German transports along the road so as not to be late for school.

Bishop Minestrini, prison chaplain in Perugia, offered invaluable help when a group of young Jews was arrested. He also helped me after that fateful 15 May when I was imprisoned by the police, by order of the notorious Prefect Rocchi.

Among the many Jews, I feel it is my duty to make special mention of Giorgio Krops, who was my good friend until his tragic death in Trieste in 1963. After he had spent some time in Assisi, this protected person became the protector of others; the saved person became the savior of others. Because of his quick intellect, he became the heart and soul of the group of Jews, together with two officers who were also in hiding at San Quirico: Colonel Gay, an Official of the High Command of the Italian Military, and Lieutenant Pilota Podda. This group worked on behalf of those who were being persecuted, especially the needy. It was they who organized the printing of the false identity cards. They continued working until the early days of May 1944, when some of them were arrested in Perugia. I cannot give first-hand evidence of anything that happened after 15 May 1944, because on that day I was also arrested. Let me to add something about that event.

It was evening, and I was returning home from the May devotions in the Church of Santo Stefano. I was met at the door of my house by two policemen in civilian dress who told me that they had orders from Prefect Rocchi to take me to Perugia. I asked them if I could please go into the house to get some things and my breviary. In my study I found Emilio and Margherita Viterbi,[4] a Jewish couple from Padua who, completely ignorant of the events happening to me, were waiting for me to come home to ask if I could please find them a new refuge because they no longer felt safe where they were staying. I told them not to move. I took my breviary and I

---

[4] The well-known Prof. Emilio Viterbi, a scientist at the University of Padua, together with his wife Margherita Levi Minzi and his daughters Grazia Benvenuta and Mirjam Rosa, had come to Assisi in October 1943.

closed the door after me, said good-bye to my parents and went off with the policemen. After ten days of confinement and a ridiculous trial based on some vague accusations I was allowed to take refuge in the Vatican, where I remained until a few days after Assisi's liberation.

Earlier I mentioned a Jew who died. I would also like to make mention of two people who were born. Maria-Enrico Finzi was born in the convent of the French Colettine Poor Clares shortly after the liberation. This family – father, mother and a three-year-old daughter – came from Belgium and were already in Assisi on 8 September 1943, so the birth of the new child was regularly reported to the police with the child's true name.

After 8 September they had been stopped several times and, in order to save them, Bishop Nicolini gave permission for the whole family to enter the cloister in Santa Coletta. That monastery had the most rigid enclosure of all the monasteries in Assisi. The Abbess at that time was Mother Helene, an exceptional woman, who had her degree from the Sorbonne. We were good friends and held each other in high esteem. For some time I had also been her confessor, but I never saw her face.

In fact, even when we met in the parlor we were separated by two grilles, behind which she frequently wore a black veil over her face. Yet with the Bishop's permission, Mother Helene let the Finzi family into the cloister. The little family lived in a single room at the end of a corridor, and little Brigitte had free range to run back and forth among the choir sisters in their work room, kitchen and chapter room. In 1964, twenty years after the little girl's birth, the monastery of the Colettine Poor Clares received a notice that M. Enrico Finzi must report for military service. However, the family had returned to Belgium after the war.

The other new baby was Francesco Clerici. He was not Jewish, but was the son of a navy officer who was in hiding in the guest house of the German Sisters of the Holy Cross where other Jews were also hidden. Officer Clerici served as our contact person in this monastery, and helped us settle in new refugees when they arrived.

For some time the Jewish writer Dino Provenzal – also sent to me by Fr. Todde – was given refuge in the monastery of the German sisters. His forged documents listed his name as Pastore, and with this name his children and the children of other Jews with false documents, attended school regularly. After the war they had their records changed.

I could continue forever, reminiscing about this period when people worked side by side for the single ideal of freedom. People of different ideas, religions, race and nationalities together imagined a bright future. We too must be heralds of peace, fighting with the same enthusiasm and faith of yesterday for fraternity among all peoples and the banishment of every type of racial or religious discrimination. This is the message we want to hand on to future generations and the whole world. Jews and Christians venerate the same book, the Bible, whose opening chapter reminds us that we are created in God's image and likeness. God is our Father, and we are all brothers and sisters.

ASSISI HERO: RESPECTED
BY CHRISTIANS AND JEWS[1]

Dinner at Casa Papa Giovanni begins promptly at 7:30. I have 15 minutes. It is late August and Assisi is uncharacteristically cool for this time of year. The streets are jammed with tourists who chose not to go to the beach for the August holidays but to visit Assisi and other hill towns in the region.

I am happy when I step into the relative solitude of the cool, travertine hallway of the Casa and the four-inch-thick, 10-foot-high door closes behind me. With only minutes to spare, I take the marble steps of the staircase two at a time to wash up before the evening meal. Memories from 20 years ago, when I first met our host, Don Aldo Brunacci, flash through my mind.

Meeting and Miracle

It is the summer of 1977, a cool morning in Assisi. Don Aldo is crossing the shaded central piazza to say Mass at the Cathedral of San Rufino. I am crossing in the opposite direction to visit the Basilica of St. Francis. I recall the morning mist burning off the plain below and the distant dome of St. Mary of the Angels shining gold against the blue Umbrian sky.

---

[1] By Susan Saint Sing in: ST. ANTHONY MESSENGER, USA, February 1999. Used with permission. One of Assisi's revered elders shares the true story of behind-the-scenes rescues that occurred in that Italian city during World War II.

As I enter the piazza, Don Aldo and I are introduced by a third man, an Australian friar named Father Thaddeus (now deceased), who is having his morning cappuccino. He jumps up from his seat at the Bar Minerva and, sidestepping the pigeons, creates an introduction that will frame the rest of my life.

He explains to Don Aldo that I am a student from America looking for work in Assisi for room-and-board in a *pensione*. Father Thaddeus then turns to me and says: "Susan, this is Don Aldo, a Canon of the Cathedral of San Rufino and the head of Casa Papa Giovanni, a major retreat house in Assisi."

Don Aldo's response stuns me. "Yes, you can come and work with us at the Casa."

A friend of mine had told me that Assisi was a magical city, so I unhesitatingly accept his offer as a miracle. After all, this is Assisi! Of course, I would find a job quickly. Nor does it seem extraordinary that I am treated as one of the family at Casa Papa Giovanni, that Don Aldo becomes a close friend who muses over my journal of drawings and fragments of poems written in Italian. He guides me on walking tours through the fields of Monte Subasio to places where he feels the true caves of St. Francis are to be found.

Don Aldo frequently tries to get me to explain to him and the Bishop of Assisi (who lives in the house) about the Church in the United States and why a twenty-two-year-old collegian would want to give up her life in the U.S. and come to Assisi.

I eventually share the story of my father's recent death, and the severe neck and back injury that brought me to Assisi to seek healing.

'Whoever Saves a Single Soul...'

Tonight, I suspect it was better that I didn't know 20 years back how great a contribution Don Aldo Brunacci has made to Assisi and the world. I now know that he was a key figure in Assisi's World War II history, the esteemed prior of the Canons of the Cathedral of San Rufino and dean of judges for the regional matrimonial tribunal.

The very year of our first meeting, on December 11, he was awarded the Medal of the Righteous Gentile from the State of Israel for his part in helping to save Jewish refugees. A Righteous Gentile is a non-Jew who risked his or her life to help save Jews. The medal Don Aldo shows his dinner guests is from the Yad Vashem Museum and Research Center in Israel and has been bestowed on more than 11,000 rescuers. He is also recognized for this action in the Holocaust Museum in Washington, D.C.

The award ceremony is a public and solemn occasion. In her book *Conscience and Courage,* historian Eva Fogelman explains: "A carob tree is planted along the Avenue of the Righteous, an avenue that leads to the museum itself, and a plaque bearing the rescuer's name and nationality marks the tree. The story of the rescuer's deed is recounted at the ceremony and filed in the museum's archives. Israeli officials then present the rescuer, or in some cases an entire rescuing group, with a medal and a certificate. The medal bears a Talmudic inscription: 'Whoever saves a single soul, it is as if he had saved the whole world.'"

One such survivor, Graziella Viterbi, still lives in Assisi. Hers was one of the Jewish families Don Aldo helped hide and relocate in Assisi. She was, in fact, in Don Aldo's house when the Nazis came to arrest him. She thanks God to this day that they did not search his residence.

I ask this modest man for details of these years of war and holocaust. Don Aldo keeps them always in his heart.

Peaceful Assisi in a Time of Peril

The Jews began to arrive in Assisi in September 1943, just after the German occupation. Many came from the north. Don

Aldo recalls: "Our first concern was to get them safely lodged in the various monasteries and convents or with reliable families who would 'forget' to comply with the police regulations to denounce any strangers in their houses. The chief center was the convent of San Quirico, where the Jewish refugees were generally housed until we could provide them with new ration books and all the papers they needed to live unmolested."

"The printing of the documents and especially the procuring of the official stamps was a difficult and risky job. All their real personal documents, as well as their sacred books and religious objects, were hidden in the cellars of the palace of the Bishop of Assisi," says the priest.

Don Aldo praises Colonel Valentin Müller, the German commandant of the occupied city of Assisi. He was a devout Catholic, devoted to St. Francis from childhood, a sympathetic man through whom Bishop Nicolini ceded to the German Medical Command many of the religious buildings in and around Assisi for the establishment of hospitals.

Don Aldo himself was arrested on May 15, 1944, and sent to a concentration camp. But on June 4, the Allies entered Rome. Don Aldo and the others imprisoned were liberated. And of course, by then the underground was no longer needed.

Putting History Right

When asked about popular films and books on this aspect of Assisi's history, Don Aldo becomes quite animated about the truth of the Holocaust. He cares nothing about recognition but, because he put his own life in harm's way to help, he has a right to see that the story gets straightened out.

The Assisi Underground, the most famous of the accounts of this period, is a dramatic fiction which places a friar in the key position. The author, Alexander Ramati, was anticipating a feature film, according to Don Aldo. But Don Aldo was there and he remembers the story somewhat differently: "The truth about the events which took place in Assisi is much more interesting than the coarse, unlikely and romanticized story which unfortunately was taken for true...."

In addition to his own remembrance, Don Aldo has documents stating that the unheralded Bishop of Assisi, Giuseppe Placido Nicolini, at the time of the war, "was the impetus, inspiration, fortitude and ecclesiastical savvy behind housing, feeding, hiding, schooling, preparing false papers for and aiding the escape of the 200 Jews hidden in the homes and monasteries of Assisi." In a parallel action, Archbishop Angelo Roncalli of Venice – later to become known as Pope John XXIII was changing birth certificates of Jews to "Catholic," securing safe passage for them out of Italy.

Why did so many Jews choose Assisi as a refuge in 1943? Don Aldo explains: "They felt drawn there by St. Francis. When the danger had passed, many told me that they attributed their safety to him."

Don Aldo becomes almost agitated and disappears into his office. He surfaces with photographs, letters and sworn documents proving that only a Bishop, not the Padre Rufino of the romanticized book-turned-film under the American title *The Assisi Underground,* could hoodwink the Nazis and pull off such a complicated, covert operation.

In the film, the Franciscan friars are given more credit for the safety of the Jews in Assisi than they were in a position to provide. It's a laughable fiction, really, since even St. Francis put himself under the local Bishop. Nothing of such magnitude could have occurred in Assisi without the Bishop spearheading it. It distresses Don Aldo, as evidenced by his direct words, that this distortion of facts – a simple friar championing the entire operation – has gained credibility and is widely accepted as true.

On June 23, 1978, Dr. Denise Pilkington of the European Editorial Office of *Reader's Digest* wrote to Don Aldo after visiting Assisi for several days to research the story of the then-newly released book describing Padre Rufino's heroism: "You will not be surprised to learn that we shall not publish that book! Because only history is worth telling."

It becomes clear to me that Don Aldo is having this candid conversation for my benefit. I understand the gravity of the issue and appreciate the quiet, organized way in which real heroes saved lives.

Son of St. Francis

Perhaps Don Aldo's rescue of Jews during the war is one reason that, behind the closed doors and walled streets of Assisi's cobblestone walks and gated houses, Don Aldo is sought out for his wisdom by families, artisans, business people and politicians.

The swarms of tourists who come to the medieval town in hope of some spiritual solace amid the kitsch of Italian shopkeepers' glow-in-the-dark "Francescoes" on a sultry August afternoon seldom see this priest. He passes unnoticed, as he prefers, calmly doing his work for Church and city and St. Francis in his own unassuming, scholarly, accurate way.

Now 91 years old, soled in black sandals, wearing black pants, usually a pale blue polyester shirt and black suit coat, he smiles easily looking over his bifocals, spryly dodging UPS trucks, as he makes his way daily between his bookshop and press, *Libreria Fonteviva,* and the Cathedral of San Rufino.

I think back to a rare evening stroll with Don Aldo and other friends. As we made our way to a concert in the town hall, progress was halting as local Assisians deferred to Don Aldo's passing, "Good evening, Don Aldo."

Babies were held for him to look at, fathers strode across the piazza to intercept him (as I now realize Father Thaddeus had done 20 years earlier on my behalf to get some private moment or answer in a quick flurry of Italian. Groups of pilgrims, everywhere in the festive streets, sometimes stopped and heads turned as guides clandestinely pointed out Don Aldo in the crowd.

I felt humble and patiently waited to the side as people jogged his memory about events of the past or appointments for the future he was to attend. "Si, si, si, si" was his standard four-syllable response. I had heard it often in our 20-year friendship.

This evening meal is two weeks before the September 1997 earthquake. During the first course of pasta and broth, green salad and bread, we dinner guests discuss politics, ostrich farms, olive trees and at rare intervals – Don Aldo himself. My mind juxtaposes the dinners from past and present and I smile. Conversation flows easily.

Don Aldo is every bit an Assisian. He was born in Assisi on April 2, 1914. His elementary schooling was in the Palazzo Locatelli, which is today the very Casa Papa Giovanni where we now dine.

Casa Papa Giovanni means *House of Pope John* and is so named for Pope John XXIII. Don Aldo speaks of Pope John and the Second Vatican Council during which the Casa's bookstore, *Libreria Fonteviva,* was founded and after which the Casa itself was donated as a religious foundation by the Diocese of Assisi.

He tells of the Church and the history of St. Francis. He recalls his appointment to travel to Baltimore to examine for authenticity a liturgical missal thought to be the actual missal once opened by St. Francis. In 1204, the Saint had asked a priest to open this missal for guidance.

Don Aldo speaks of changing times as a local, as one born and raised here: how dear the houses and the land are to buy, and how Assisi has become so replete with shops and souvenirs that he welcomes people now, tongue in cheek, to the town of Francis' merchant father, Pietro Bernardone, instead of Francesco Bernardone himself.

Don Aldo goes on to talk about how Assisi through the ages has been the spinal cord of strategic military importance with travel up and down the axis of Italy, from Roman legions to Napoleon in 1797-1798 housing his army's horses in the Basilica of St. Mary of the Angels and deporting the Bishop of Assisi and some of the parish priests to France! I am reminded that Don Aldo Brunacci is not only a part of history but a scholar of history in his own right. He is a Latin and Greek classicist, who brings his immense classical learning to his understanding of Assisi's and Italy's history.

He worries about the *Casa*, an institute of religious hospitality, a center of Franciscan study and retreat with its two libraries, a classroom, chapel, elevator, roof garden, solar panels on the roof, olive trees, roses, zinnias, balconies constructed trellis-like up the hillside with porticoes of travertine and ceilings of Renaissance frescoes. The rooms for pilgrims cover three floors and are surprisingly spartan: a cell, with a modest desk, bed and chair.

The views of Perugia, the plain, the fortress above the city and the serenity in the roof garden are cuddled beneath terra cotta roof tiles and cool plaster walls. It is an oasis in the Umbrian heat, above the racket of the constant flow of walkers-by, delivery trucks and horns on Via San Paolo.

The hour grows late and Assisi's bells peal under the black sky and etched stars. A modern troubadour's guitar-strums, accompanied by six or seven voices, reverberate through the courtyard. Don Aldo remembers, "When I was a young cleric, I rode my bike everywhere throughout the diocese. All through the countryside the farmers would be singing, too, and working to the songs. Different songs for different work." He says: "Assisi has always been a place where people feel free to sing."

I ask Don Aldo what he wishes to see in the next millennium. He says without hesitation, "Peace." He is indeed the servant of St. Francis. He is a churchman of honor and rank, equivalent to a monsignor, yet he wears no red, drives his own car, walks about town, assumes no airs. He speaks of peace as a man who has lived through war, as a man who was imprisoned for his part in aiding Jews and refugees in Assisi during the war.

As dinner comes to a close, with the table strewn with pages of files and news clippings, photos from Israel, linen napkins, vino, cameras and quiet glances sealed in nods, hugs and hushed Italian, I know that this evening is about to end.

We have been talking since 7:30 p.m. and it is now nearly 11. As we walk through the roof garden gate and turn to face the hill's night coolness sweetened by ginestra, we silently muse over the complex recollections Don Aldo has just shared with us.

I am rapt in the magic of Assisi: a tapestry from ancient Rome to the Middle Ages to the present, artfully woven by a true troubadour and son of St. Francis, Don Aldo Brunacci.

IN ASSISI
NOT ONE WAS TOUCHED[1]

Who can possibly write the account of such charity, in our city, Assisi, according to the prophecy of St. Francis, has never before been refuge and salvation, both physical and spiritual, for so many people as it was during this conflict?

We must remember two important dates: July 25, 1943, which saw the fall of the Fascist regime, and September 8, 1943, the day when the government broke off its alliance with Hitler and took sides with the Allied forces.

In retaliation for this affront the Germans occupied central and northern Italy, including Rome and Assisi. Only the most fanatical Fascists sided with them, becoming very dangerous spies. As a result, the Bishop's residence became the only center of assistance for those who were flowing into Assisi to escape both from the cities that were being bombed and from the war front, which was getting closer every day. It was then that the assistance committee, headed by the Bishop, came into existence; it continued unto the end of the war. This committee sheltered an immigrant population that at one point was as large as the population of Assisi itself.

---

[1] *Italian Priest Remembers Holocaust Heroism* in: JEWISH STANDARD, June 7, 2002. Used with permission.

Editors' note: On April 26, Father Aldo Brunacci spoke at Temple Emanuel of the Pascack Valley in Woodcliff Lake. These are edited exerpts from his talk.

Some Jewish families had arrived in Assisi even before September 8 but after this date, even more arrived. One day that month, the Bishop called me aside and said: "We must get organized to help those who are persecuted and above all the Jews. All must be done with the utmost discretion and reserve. No one, not even the clergy, must know about this."

With the Bishop's help, a center where refugees arrived from war-devastated countries already had opened; it was not difficult to work within that large organization to help Jews. The Bishop's residence in Assisi is large, with large cellars. Often both people and their belongings had to be hidden – there were things that were inherently precious and others that held precious memories. These precious objects were hidden in the cellars, and the cellars were walled off. This task was not to be entrusted to regular bricklayers, so it was the Bishop himself who took trowel to hand while I held up a candle to light his work. When there was digging to be done we changed places; I dug and he held the candle. When people had to leave the center before the war's end, the work had to be undone, their belongings removed, and the cellar sealed again.

After September 8, more Jews arrived; their numbers swelled again after the German occupation was firmly consolidated. They came from Trieste, Padua, and Milan; from France, Austria, and Yugoslavia. Although the Bishop's residence was our organization's headquarters, the refugees were placed at the Convent of St. Quirico and in the guest rooms of Santa Croce, the German Capuchin Sisters' convent. They remained there until they were given false identity cards, which were necessary because without them the refugees could not receive ration cards. With these new papers, our guests were able to live undisturbed, even in hotels or private apartments.

Printing the documents was a difficult and risky job; it was even harder and more risky to make the rubber stamps. Among the people who helped us was a firmly anti-Fascist typographer who had a small, pedal-driven printing press (which can be found today in a souvenir shop not far from the Basilica of St. Clare).

Even with faked identity cards, people still had to be very careful. One young lady, who according to her made-up identity card was from Bari, answered her interlocutors with a Venetian accent. Her presence of mind, combined with the instructions she'd been given, saved her; she insisted that she'd picked up the accent because she'd studied in Venice.

One evening, a man of Polish descent who had always lived in France, his wife, and their children arrived in Assisi; they'd escaped from a French concentration camp and crossed the Alps on foot. None of them spoke Italian. The diocese of Genoa sent them to Florence and then on to Assisi. The secretary of the Archbishop of Genoa gave them false papers that said they were Italians returning from French-speaking Tunisia. We found shelter for them with the French Poor Clares; until they received their ration cards we hid them in a small apartment above a hayloft, reachable only by ladder.

A Russian family was housed in the convent and so was a Belgian family named Finzi. The Finzis arrived in Assisi before the Germans occupied it, so they had been registered. Therefore, the police came to get them, but they were not at home. The convent's abbess immediately got the Bishop's permission to hide the family in the cloister, a place so sacred the police did not dare violate it. After the liberation, a baby, Enrico Finzi, was born in the convent.

An elderly Viennese lady died in the convent of St. Quirico; other refugees worried about her burial. "Don't worry," I said to them, "I'll take care of everything without raising the least suspicion." I went to the municipal authorities and bought a burial niche; I told them it was for a refugee who had left me money to do so. I escorted the coffin to the cemetery, and a German patrol passed by respectfully, never guessing that under the funeral pall was a Jew. She was buried as Bianca Bianchi, the name she'd been using in Assisi. After liberation, her son, who had gone to Brazil, came to find her grave. We put her real name, along with a star of David, on a new tombstone.

We incurred many dangers and had to constantly move refugees because we were afraid our neighbors were getting suspicious. Some pastors helped us find new hiding places; Rev. Federico Vincenti hid some young Jewish men in Perugia. Sometimes I would sleep in the refugees' shelters; I would leave Assisi at sundown by bicycle and ride back in time for school. If it was late, I would hold on to the back of a German military transport truck.

One day the police came to my door, just when Prof. Emilio Viterbi and his wife, Margherita, Jews from Padua, were in my study. They wanted me to find them a new, safer place to live. I reassured the Viterbis, closed the study door, said goodbye to my parents, and went with the police, who did not search my parents' house. I was confined in a makeshift concentration camp in Perugia, and told that my fate would be decided by Prefect Rocchi, a Fascist leader who collaborated with the Germans. Fortunately, by that time the Allies were just outside Rome, which was liberated on June 4. I was able to escape to Rome and find shelter in the Vatican.

When the Jews were in Assisi I developed a real, fraternal friendship with them, their faith, and their culture, based on mutual esteem and respect. I shall never forget the deep emotion I felt on October 8, 1943, when a large group of Jews of different nationalities gathered in a room in the convent to celebrate Yom Kippur. The nuns had decorated the refectory and the tables with flowers. When the guests sat down for the meal, the nuns decided to serve the meal that closed their own penitential day. The guests no longer felt like strangers; they looked one another in the eye and understood that they had been received as brothers and sisters.

At the end of the war, Dr. Renzo Levi, representing a group of refugees, wrote to Bishop Nicolini. His letter read: "Even here in Rome, the ecclesiastical organizations were lavish in their help and advice, but the work of Your Excellency turned out to be particularly worthy of gratitude because... we were happy to learn that not one of our refugees lost his life in Assisi, nor was there any deportation, as, unfortunately, was the case more than once here in Rome."

In a testimonial he delivered on January 6, 1946, for Bishop Nicolini's 70th birthday, Prof. Viterbi wrote: "We shall always tell our children and every one else... during a persecution that annihilated 6 million Jews... in Assisi not one was touched!"

May this be an example of the real brotherhood that should unite all mankind.

FROM A COURAGEOUS
YOUTH OF YESTERDAY

A TESTIMONY OF FAITH, HUMANITY,
AND PEACE FOR THE YOUTH OF TODAY[1]

Often certain honors are given to people and organizations out of mere window dressing, for they have a great name, but have accomplished nothing. But recently that was not the case. For the authority standing behind the honor and the person receiving the recognition were outstanding. We are referring to The Day of Remembrance celebrated on January 27 in Italy to remember the persecution and extermination of the Jews in the Nazi concentration camps during World War II. On that occasion the President of the Italian Republic, Carlo Azeglio Ciampi officially conferred the honor of Knight of the Great Cross, upon Don Brunacci, a priest of Assisi, today a nonagenerian, for the support, assistance, and solidarity shown the refugees and persecuted Jews during the last tragic years of the war.

During those years of blood and violence as the Germans and Anglo-Americans fought in Italy people stepped forward in the name of human and Christian solidarity to protect and save so many human lives, at personal risk and without marking any distinction with regard to faith or nationality. Among these courageous and generous benefactors was Don Aldo

---

[1] A Conversation in Assisi with Don Aldo Brunacci, originally published in L'OSSERVATORE ROMANO, February 8, 2003, p. 11, by Mario Spinelli. Used with permission.

Brunacci, who worked together with Bishop Guiseppe Placido Nicolini, the Bishop of Assisi during those years, and hid hundreds of Jews, whether Italians or foreigners, during house searches, thus saving them from deportation and certain death.

The festive occasion of this high honor gave Don Aldo a chance to take another and deeper look at the events of those tragic and courageous years.

Between 1943-1945 the Italian Church – bishops and priests, religious men and sisters and ordinary faithful, convents and Catholic organization – were in the first line of providing aid and concrete solidarity with all those who were suffering and at greatest risk because of this brutal conflict. It was an historical event now recognized by all. The Great Cross, given to Don Brunacci by the highest authority within the government, is a symbolic expression of the valued acknowledgment of the entire nation and the Italian people to the Church and to the Catholic world for what they did during these bloody years.

We spoke about these and other matters with Don Aldo (still youthful and full of vigor despite his advanced age) in his native Assisi, in the Bishop's house which was the scene of many dramatic acts of heroism on his part and that of Bishop Nicolini. Don Aldo's reactions, answers, and reflections fully reveal him in all his simplicity, modesty, humility, but full of candor. This elderly hero has preserved all the idealism and purity of his intrepid youth.

Beloved Don Brunacci, first of all let's speak of the effect upon you of receiving such a high honor from the first citizen of your country.

Truthfully, I've only received a telegram from the General Secretary of the President of the Republic, telling me of the honor to be conferred on me. At the present time I don't know when the celebration will take place. Certainly I'm a little surprised and pleased at the same time. Indeed the message from the ministry did not specify the reasons, and at the beginning I was uncertain why I was being honored. I thought that perhaps someone was pulling my leg. But I still remain pleased, also thinking of all the time that has passed by – now sixty years.

What recollections do you have to those events?

I remember the events very well. I was young, thirty years of age. The images are permanently stamped on my mind. It was a very hectic period. And it's a good thing that we are having this interview here in the Bishop's house, for Bishop Nicolini was the heart and center of all the activities for assistance and aid. After July 25, 1943 it had fallen to him to take control of so many civic responsibilities, since the civil authorities had abandoned ship. In the Bishop's house a large committee was established. The Bishop was its president, and I was its secretary.

More than 4,000 refugees came to Assisi from cities bombed in the South, and we tried to arrange things for them the best we could. But after September 8 we added the work of assisting those being persecuted by the government, especially the Jews. One day Bishop Nicolini showed me a letter from the Secretary of State in which the Vatican recommended that we give maximum assistance to those who were being persecuted, above all to the Jews. When the Jewish families began to arrive in large numbers, we first turned to the Basilica of San Francesco and to the Sacro Convento, which were the natural places to go.

So you collaborated with the Franciscan friars?

The sacristan, Father Todde, is well remembered from this point of view because he sent me some Jewish refugee families for me to take care of. But the Sacro Convento was too obvious a hiding place. Instead they hid the Jewish families in the guest rooms of other friaries and monasteries – with the

German Sisters, the Franciscan Colettine nuns, the Sisters of San Quirico, the Holy Cross Sisters, the Stigmatines and so many others. I also placed them with many private families, whom I trusted.

Furthermore, we provided the refugees with a new identity, giving them new names and documents, making them hail from a city in Italy where there weren't many Germans. A movie was made of these events, *Assisi Underground,* with Jews dressed as friars and other things of that sort. But it was a distortion of that page of history.

Where you afraid, Father? When was it the most risky?

But look at what I've already said and what I repeat every chance I get. The one who deserves the credit for all these works is above all my Bishop at that time. The Knight of the Great Cross should have been given to his memory. In 1977 when I was honored with the title of The Just of Israel and invited to Jerusalem to plant a tree in The Park of the Just, I said that I would accept only if they gave the same honor first of all to Bishop Nicolini. So I went to Jerusalem together with his successor, Bishop Dino Tomassini, who was declared Just of Israel in the name and in the memory of his predecessor. And each one of us planted his own tree.

Your own modesty and your dedication to the memory of your Bishop bring honor to you, Don Aldo. But without your own courage and work would the head of the diocese have had a voice and been able to perform his works of charity and solidarity? Weren't you the more visible and the more vulnerable diocesan worker?

Sure, that's so. I had no fear nor did I think of the risks I was running. I thought only that I was fighting for a just cause and that was enough to give me courage and perseverance. I was only concerned about my parents, because in those months Assisi was full of spies for OVRA[2]. The Germans had other things to think about, and pressed into service Fascist collaborators and militia. Finally, one day Bishop Nicolini showed me a pack of photos – I don't know how he got them – in which I had been photographed talking with people in all sectors of Assisi. Clearly it was the work of OVRA. And in fact on May 15 of 1944 I found the police at my door.

And what happened?

They carted me off to Perugia and to a make-ready and hostile tribunal, composed of collaborators and militia of the Republic of Salò. They accused me of ridiculous and incredible things. Since they could not touch the Bishop, they leveled all their attacks at me. They threatened to deport me to Germany, but there was no time, for the Allies were making great advances. They put me into a Perugian school that functioned as a concentration camp and I managed to escape to Rome.

How many Jews did you save?

Since I never kept an exact count, I cannot answer your question with any precision. But between Assisi and its outskirts we assuredly are dealing with no less than 300.

One final question, Father. You saved so many Jews during World War II and were a Catholic priest. During these days there is criticism of Pope Pius XII that he didn't do enough for the persecuted and refugee Jews at the same time that you were doing so much, but kept a culpable silence. What's your thought about this matter?

---

[2] Editors' note: Don Aldo Brunacci remembers them as secret police.

I respond with a recent event. Last year I was in the USA, invited by two universities (St. Francis in Brooklyn, NY and St. Bonaventure University in Olean, NY) and three synagogues. In Buffalo I met with the council of the Jewish community of that city. The television people were there and asked so many questions. Of course, one of the questions touched on the presumed silence of Pius XII.

I first answered with another question: Tell me: Is it better to speak or to do? And after I got the response naturally, to do, I cited studies and documents which calculated that Pius XII saved from deportation and death at least 800,000 Jews. For the rest, I have already mentioned the letter from the Vatican Secretary of State, dated September 1943, asking Bishop Nicolini to protect the refugees and in particular the Jews. But there is more. There are entire volumes – the Jesuits have worked very much in this area – which demonstrate the solidarity and specific actions taken by Pope Pacelli in defense of the Jews persecuted by the Nazis.

JEWISH REFUGEES[1]

In a recent number of the Catholic Times I noticed a paragraph about Jews in Assisi during the war. The details had been transmitted to the National Catholic Welfare Conference of America by the Rabbi R.E. Resnik, director in Italy of the Committee of American Assistance to the Jews. And as I was personally involved in the work of protecting these persecuted people, I thought it might be of interest to English readers to know how we carried out our efforts.

The Jews began to arrive in Assisi in September 1943, after the German occupation. Many of them came from the north and I often asked them why so many chose Assisi as a refuge, for it is a place with no record of any Jewish citizens.

Nearly always I received the answer that they felt drawn there by Saint Francis, and when the danger had passed many told me that they attributed their safety to him.

A boy who had been one of our most useful collaborators during the worst time wrote to his mother: "I was protected by Our Lady and Saint Francis." They were both Jews, but she sent me the boy's letter.

With every encroachment of the German occupation more Jews arrived, and our first thought was, to get them safely lodged in the various convents and with reliable families who

---

[1] This article was written by Don Aldo Brunacci in 1946. Used with permission. The book *The Assisi Underground* (American title) or *While the Pope Kept Silent* (English title) is a false representation of the facts, a work of the imagination, not even loosely related to the true happenings.

would forget to comply with the police regulations of denouncing any strangers they had in the house.

Still, in a small place the presence of so many visitors was bound to be noted, even though Assisi then had a considerable number of non-Jewish refugees from other parts of Italy.

We felt that our Jewish friends must be protected. We provided them with false identity cards to pass them off as refugees from places already occupied by the Allies. Our chief center was the convent of San Quirico, where the visitors were generally housed until we could provide them with new ration books and all the papers which were necessary to enable them to live unmolested. Armed with these documents some of them lived with immunity in an ordinary hotel.

The printing of the documents and especially making official stamps was a difficult and risky job, but it was managed and we obtained ration books through the help of trusted friends.

When the documents and a "covering" story were ready, our refugees had to learn the geography of their "new" home, and were primed with every detail about local habits, personalities and gossip.

It was more difficult to provide them with the right accent and intonation and a young lady from Bari supprised hearers by answering their question in pure Venetian. Her presence of mind, however, rose to the occasion and she coolly told them of her education and upbringing in the north.

One evening a father, mother and son arrived who had escaped from a concentration camp in France. They knew no Italian and were in fact pure French. They had crossed the Alps on foot, and had been helped by the Curia in Genoa which forwarded them on to Florence whence they had been sent to Assisi for greater safety.

The secretary of the archbishop of Genoa had already provided them with documents declaring that they were Italian refugees repatriated from Tunis so we only had to find them lodging and clothes and within a week our French friends were going about quite happily and no one suspected them.

We had a difficult case in the convent when an old lady of Vienesse Jewish origin died, and it was necessary to bury her without a Catholic funeral and yet not arouse suspicion. However that, too, was managed and Madame Weiss now rests in the cemetery of Assisi under the name of Signora Bianchi.

We were particularly anxious that the Jewish boys and girls should not waste their time and, thanks to their false papers, several of them continued their studies in the public schools, while others were prepared privately and then presented themselves in the usual manner for the state examination, at which they did very well. After the liberation, of course, we corrected their names in the school records.

The idea that the Jews made a synagogue in the crypt of the very monastery founded by Saint Francis is misleading, for there is no monastery in Assisi founded by Saint Francis, and there was no synagogue in any crypt.

But it is true that in the quiet of the Assisi convents, the Jews were naturally completely free to join together for their devotions, and it often happened that while the nuns were at their prayers, close at hand, under the same roof, the Jews, too, were imploring the Divine mercy and asking God for justice and peace.

I remember how, just after the Jews had begun to arrive in Assisi on October 8, 1943, they were celebrating their Feast of Yom Kippur in the convent of San Quirico, a quiet hidden celebration of refugees. The sisters, however, had the happy inspiration of decorating the refectory and tables with flowers as for a feast and when their guests sat down to the meal after the long ritual fast and looked round, they no longer felt like strangers and understood that in the bond of charity we are all brothers and sisters.

It would take too long to tell of our many anxieties while trying to help those whom Providence sent us during those hard years. Our organization had ramifications in some of the small neighboring places, for we did not want too many visitors to Assisi itself. We were, of course, in connection with other curias, for practically all the Italian clergy were working on similar lines as ourselves. Our organization was not large, but we found that our measures worked efficiently.

All the personal documents – the real ones – of our Jews, as well as their sacred books and religious objects were hidden the cellars of the palace of the Bishop of Assisi, and from beginning to end he was the heart and soul of our work, which continued until the liberation.

When I was arrested as suspect on May 15, 1944 I had a Jewish couple hidden in my house, and we were preparing the means of escape for their relations in northern Italy. I was sent to a concentration camp where other Jews were interned, but on June 4 the Allies entered Rome, and our help was no longer needed.

In all, about two hundred Jews had been entrusted to us by Divine Providence. With God's help, and through the intercession of Saint Francis, not one of them fell into the hands of their persecutors.

STORIA MEDICINALI

A PERSONAL NOTE BY BISHOP NICOLINI[1]

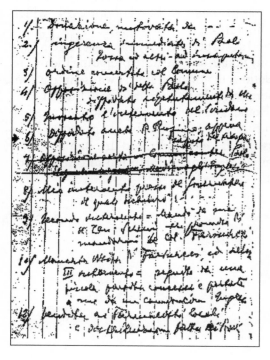

This autograph of Bishop Nicolini is clear proof that Fr. Rufino had no rapport with the Bishop. In this note the Bishop declares that he mistrusts (*Diffidato*) Fr. Rufino.[2]

"*...3. Ordine concertato col Comune.*

4. Opposizione di detto Paolo... diffidato ripetutamente da me...

6. **Diffidato** *anche P. Rufino, appena saputo del trasferimento. ...*"

---

[1] Bishop Nicolini's autograph from the diocesan archives. Used with permission.

[2] See Santucci, pp. 105-107.

DR. VALENTIN MÜLLER

BIOGRAPHICAL NOTES[1]

Valentin Müller was born in 1891 at Zeilitzheim, lower Franconia in Bavaria. An uncle-priest encouraged him to attend the *Kilianeum*, the minor seminary at Würzburg in 1904. In 1911 having finished the *Gymnasium* he started his medical studies in this beautiful cathedral city. During World War I he served as doctor and was honored with a silver medal for bravery (similar to a knight's cross). He was imprisoned by the British army, but later liberated by exchange. After the war he completed his studies and settled in 1919 as a medical doctor at Titting.

At the outbreak of World War II, Müller had a medical practice in Eichstätt, Oberbayern, approximately 100 km (60 miles) north of Munich. He had moved there in 1933 because he had experienced difficulties with the Nazis in nearby Titting.

In 1939, again in the military, he was elevated to the rank of Colonel and took part in the campaigns against Poland, France and Russia. In Stalingrad in 1942 he was said to have

---

[1] By Josef Raischl: The following observations are taken from his daughter Irmgard's travel journal as well as conversations with family members and contemporaries. His children, Irmgard and Robert, both eventually became physicians. They learned very little from him personally about what happened during his time in Assisi because he was very reticent about his experiences during the war and recorded only what was necessary in his written works. Moreover, Valentin Müller died rather young on 31 July 1951, in his sixtieth year.

established the first military hospital. Several days before the Red Army surrounded the city, Müller was sent to Lourdes, the pilgrimage sanctuary in southern France. There he had to establish a division for medical transport. As head of that division he arrived in Italy in 1943.

While he was serving as representative of the head of the medical corps for the army in southern Italy as chief of staff, he learned of the general's plan to establish a military hospital in Assisi, a plan in which he immediately expressed interest. Thus he became director of the hospital which would eventually care for some 200 sick and wounded. Still later he would be named commander of the city of Assisi.

In the interim he was named *Oberstarzt*, a rank which is usually reserved for doctors who also teach medicine. His extraordinary energy and his organizational skill seem to have predestined him for this job. In later years his own son would describe him as a "super-active man, going everywhere at once." Whatever we know about his activity in Assisi, we know primarily from the citizens themselves. The *Colonello* was esteemed and loved. He fostered good relationships with Mayor Fortini and Bishop Nicolini. He was at home with the Franciscans. Everyone knew that whatever their need, the *Colonello* would have an ear for it. Everyone knew his telephone number at the command post: 210. The good doctor tried with all his might to prevent any encroachment on the part of his own countrymen. When he failed to do so, he made a personal effort to repair the harm.

Once two German officers confiscated two taxis. Müller mounted his motorcycle and followed the two officers all the way to Perugia where he apprehended the two of them and constrained them to return the vehicles. Francesco Pettirossi, one of the two taxi drivers, never forgot the *Colonello*.

Another time German soldiers confiscated all the bicycles they found and loaded them onto a truck. Only when Müller commanded them to do so did the soldiers unload the truck and return the bicycles. One night he ran to help a young woman and her children who were being harassed by drunken soldiers. And at risk to himself, he helped the young wife of an Italian interred in a German concentration camp get a letter to her husband. He took her letter and put it in an envelope with his own name on it as the sender. At the hospital he not only treated wounded soldiers but also cared for the sick and injured without cost. He even made house calls!

The high esteem in which the people held him can be seen in the fact that the resistance fighters in the area around Assisi were told: "Don't touch a hair of Colonel Müller's head."

Before withdrawing from Assisi on 17 June 1944, he arranged to have all the medical provisions – general supplies, medicine, beds, blankets and all kinds of surgical equipment worth approximately 10,000,000 lire – given to the Bishop of Assisi for him to distribute.[2] To be precise about it, on Thursday, 15 June 1944, Müller gathered the Bishop and representatives of the city government in the Hotel Subasio to thank them for their hospitality. He is reported to have said: "Now at the height of reprisals people are tempted to regard as traitors anyone who supported the opposite side." Once again he risked life and limb. Unfortunately, the ultimate fate of these supplies is still not clear, but it seems that when the city was liberated, the International Red Cross apparently confiscated it all, despite considerable protest from Bishop Nicolini. Don Aldo Brunacci reports that Father Rufino Nicacci, at that time the guardian of San Damiano, had a role to play in the matter:

> Rufino Nicacci is the leading character in Ramati's book, *Assisi Underground*. This is pure fiction. The author was obviously planning on a screenplay, and with this purpose in mind he could not have found a protagonist more suitable and imaginative than Fr. Rufino.

---

[2] See Santucci, 103-112, *La Questione dei Medicinali.*

At the end of the occupation of Assisi Fr. Rufino, together with a Slovak Jew by the name of Pavel Jotza, was involved in an action that was anything but judicious. I am referring to the enormous supply of medical equipment that Colonel Müller so courageously and generously had given to the people of Assisi. He loved and protected our city. Father Rufino and Jotza were warned against their action by Bishop Nicolini. The hand-written text of this warning appears on p. 108 of Santucci's book.

His final act was to leave behind a letter asking his opponents to respect the dignity of the city. He also had posters with this message affixed to various places throughout the city.

After being released from American imprisonment in 1945, he returned to Eichstätt and continued his practice until his death in 1951. He died of lung cancer which travelled to his brain within a few weeks in a hospital at Munich, and was buried in the cemetery of Eichstätt.

Finally, in 1982 during a pilgrimage for the 800th anniversary of the birth of St. Francis, a delegation from Assisi visited Colonel Müller's grave in Eichstätt. A view of the Basilica of St. Francis in Assisi with the Sacro Convento is carved on the headstone. Above it is a Latin inscription: *In serviendo consumor* (*I give my life in serving.*).

COLONEL VALENTIN MÜLLER, MD[1]

It was a hot and humid July 31, 1990 when Don Aldo Brunacci, director of the Casa Papa Giovanni and Prior of the Canons of the Cathedral of San Rufino, invited me to an evening Eucharist in the Casa chapel. After working all day with the pilgilms making The Assisi Experience, I was tired and not up to attending another mass. However, when I arrived in the chapel, I changed my mind when I saw several of the anziani *or senior citizens of Assisi gathered. They gathered to remember, to remember fondly Dr. Valentin Müller on the anniversary of his death. They call him, with great respect, the savior of Assisi during World War II.*

Having visited Dr. Müller's family in Eichstatt several times, it was during my last visit that Robert Müller's son-in-law, Josef Raischl, translated this article from German. I have edited it and offer it as another picture of Assisi during World War II and of Dr. Valentin Müller. It fits well with the tribute paid to Dr. Müller by the people of Assisi in the memorial they have erected in his honor, seen on a city wall as one comes up the road to Assisi. One cannot miss it, for it is at the crossroads of two gates leading into the city.

"Daddy went on alone to the Hotel Subasio. The desk clerk recognized him instantly and excitedly called the proprietors, Mr. and Mrs. Rossi. It was a wonderful welcome

---

[1] By André Cirino and Josef Raischl in: THE CORD, January 1992, *Assisi in World War II.* Used with permission.

from a grateful people." In these words from her travel journal, Irmgard Müller, daughter of Dr. Valentin Müller, describes her father's return to Assisi in 1950. Just six years after the departure of the German army, the former Medical Colonel and Commander of Assisi, returned to the city of Francis and Clare for a visit.

Ironically, the former occupier and enemy is practically given a hero's welcome just a few short years after the war. The former Mayor, who was in office during Müller's time, the present communist Mayor and the Bishop received him. Müller received numerous invitations from the citizens of Assisi to come visit. Upon his arrival, some women placed flowers at the hotel entrance that formerly served as his headquarters. Now he and his family are invited guests of the Hotel Subasio. And the City Council wants to erect a monument in his honor.

Dr. Valentin Müller's presence is celebrated in the streets and squares of the city. People crowded around him, shaking his hand, embracing him. Why this adulation of a former Nazi occupier? Let the people's stories and personal experience of the Commander explain why. In her travel journal Irmgard Müller wrote: "A woman approached us, happy and very moved, to share of the *grande paura* – the great fear – she had during the war. But when *Il Colonnello* moved into the city, the fear left her. The inhabitants of Assisi revere Müller as the city's savior. They claim it is due to his presence that the city's sanctuaries, medieval walls, treasures as well as its inhabitants, remained untouched. During the war the people used to exclaim: "We've got three protectors: God, St. Francis, and Colonel Müller."

Concerning the details of Müller's assignment in Assisi, he himself said very little. "My father never boasted of his heroic deeds," says his son Robert Müller, MD, who continued his father's medical practice in Eichstätt together with his own son Dominic. For the most part he was a man of few words who wrote even less. Moreover, he had only a short time to live, for on 31 July 1951, he died at the age of 60. Therefore, what we have gathered about his presence in Assisi comes mainly from the people of Assisi themselves.

At the beginning of World War II, Müller was working as a doctor in Eichstätt, about 60 miles from Munich. He moved there in 1933 because of problems he had with the local Nazi authorities in a nearby village called Titting. As a medical student, Müller served in World War I. He was awarded the Bavarian Silver Medal for bravery for saving some injured soldiers at the front line. So in 1939 he was called to war again, this time as a surgeon and captain. He participated in expeditions in Poland, France and Russia. In Stalingrad he was supposed to set up the first hospital in 1942. Just a few days before a Russian army surrounded the city, Müller was transferred to Lourdes to establish a medical transport unit. And as its chief he later came to Italy in 1943.

While he was replacing the Medical General of the troops of southern Italy, he heard about the general's plan to establish Assisi as a hospital city. Müller succeeded in getting himself assigned to Assisi as Commander, later receiving more than 2,000 sick and injured people. Because of his extraordinary energy and organizational ability, Müller was promoted to the rank of colonel, a rank in the health corp ordinarily restricted to professors of medicine. His son Robert describes him as "a courageous, active, no, a super-active man who was part of everything."

When Müller took up his assignment in February, 1944, the closest Allied position was at Anzio, 110 miles south of Assisi. At that time, cities of ecclesiastical and cultural significance like Assisi were not considered neutral or exempt from war. The Benedictine Abbey of Montecassino, a cultural monument comparable to Assisi, was completely destroyed in 1944. Moreover, Assisi was strategically important because of the nearby airports of Foligno and Perugia.

Very early in the war years the Conventual friars of Assisi appealed to their General Minister in Rome, Bede Hess, who, with the support of the papal curia and Bishop Placido Nicolini of Assisi, approached both sides in the conflict asking them not to touch the city. On 10 July 1943, the President of the United States, Franklin D. Roosevelt, declared his country's intention not to touch the Vatican nor its possessions (which according to the Lateran Pact included some ecclesiastical buildings in Assisi). Later on, Arnaldo Fortini, Mayor of Assisi, contacted the Allied forces and received assurance from Field Marshall Alexander, their Commander, that Assisi would be preserved.

The German army was not willing to do the same. Müller immediately tried to cut through the red tape to get the status of either a hospital city or open city for Assisi, according to international law. According to the Geneva Convention of the Red Cross, no fighting forces were allowed in a hospital city. The law of the Hague ordered that all military personnel must be removed from an open city. All of this must be accepted by both sides. But the German headquarters in Berlin delayed such a declaration until the front line approached the city in question, thus trying to avoid tactical disadvantages. So Müller's first efforts were in vain.

The Medical Colonel then took matters into his own hands. He sent the remaining troops out of the city, locked the gates at night, and placed guards as well as signs on the gates and walls to keep the withdrawing German troops from entering. Müller did not have the authority to act as he did. Nevertheless, the Colonel's persistence finally paid off. On 1 June 1944, von Kessel from the German embassy advised the Vatican that Assisi was declared a hospital city. The German Ambassador to the Vatican, Ernst von Weizsäcker and the German Commander in Italy, Field Marshall Albert Kesselring, concurred. So Assisi was left untouched when on 16 June 1944, the German Army retreated. Müller, the last one to leave, posted signs all over the city as well as leaving behind a letter to the Allied forces (the British were first to enter Assisi), pleading with them to respect the city's dignity.

Colonel Müller was respected and loved by the citizens of Assisi. As Commander, he cared for St. Francis' city. He had a good rapport with Bishop Nicolini and Mayor Fortini. He frequently visited the friars. Everyone knew that *Il Colonnello* would listen to them, their problems, or injustices experienced. Desperate people would telephone him at his office for everyone knew his number, 210. Müller tried to stop the German soldiers from exploiting the people, and if he could not, he personally worked for reparation of the damages.

For example, one day two German captains commandeered two taxis, pretending there was an emergency. Müller himself followed them by motorcycle and caught up with them near Perugia. He had them return the stolen cars. After many years, Francesco Pettirossi, one of the taxi owners, has never forgotten and enthusiastically tells his guests about *Il Colonnello* who brought his taxi back to him. Another time German soldiers started to confiscate bicycles, loading them on a truck. Only *Il Colonnello's* order stopped them. And one night, Müller helped a woman and her two children who were being taunted by drunken soldiers. And to a young wife of an Italian soldier who was in a German concentration camp, *Il Colonnello* gave her the possibility of contacting him. Müller put her letter into an official envelope from his office, making himself, at great risk, the sender.

In the city hospitals *Il Colonnello* treated not only the injured soldiers, but freely treated the poor, attending them in emergency – even in their homes. Before the Germans withdrew, Müller ordered that all medical equipment – medicine, beds, surgical instruments, etc. worth ten million lire – be left to the Bishop of Assisi for distribution. Müller was aware of the danger he incurred by aiding the enemy. He is supposed to have said: "Now at the peak of (German) oppression, people will be fast to judge as traitors those who helped the enemy." And the great esteem Müller had among the people was evidenced by the announcement of the partisans near Assisi, that upon withdrawal: "*Colonnello* Müller will not be harmed!"

Just as in other territories occupied by the Germans, the Jews were persecuted. In Italy about 32,000 Jews survived in hidden places, about 300 of them in monasteries and private homes in Assisi. Did Colonel Müller know about them? "I suppose so," says Robert Müller, the Colonel's son, "and if he was deceived, then it was because he wanted to be deceived." Robert Müller was asked: what would your father have done if he would have known? "Nothing, he would have allowed it because he looked at the Jews the same way he looked at all people." It is also known that in 1937, Dr. Valentin Müller bought his house from a Jewish family and paid for it immediately with cash, thus giving them the means to escape. Moreover, Müller was the last medical doctor in Eichstätt to visit Jewish homes for treatment.

In 1984 the Jewish director Alexander Ramati, who once came to Assisi as an Allied war Journalist, made a movie on the Jews saved by the people of Assisi. The film, shot at original sites in Assisi, had Maximilian Schell portray Müller. Schell once said he would never again accept the role of a German officer in a film. Yet, getting to know some of Müller's person and character, he accepted the role. Robert Müller claims his father is portrayed as "too slow and sedate, respectable, but not seeing through the situation." In Robert's opinion, his father was much more vivacious and flexible than the film portrayed.

The memory of *Il Colonnello's* important role in preserving Assisi during World War II is still alive among the city's inhabitants. In 1982, a commemorative stone monument was placed in the cloister of the Würzburg Conventual friary, bearing the names of Mayor Fortini, Father Bede Hess, Bishop

Nicolini and Dr. Valentin Müller. It was brought by a delegation from Assisi on a pilgrimage of peace during the eighth centennary of St. Francis' birth to the first Franciscan friary established north of the Alps. On their way the group also stopped at Eichstätt. After a reception at the City Hall, the Italians brought olive branches to Colonel Müller's grave, on whose tombstone the facade of the Basilica of San Francesco is carved. Above are the words: *In serviendo consumor* (*I give my life in serving*).

REMEMBERING COMPASSION
DURING WAR[1]

For more than 700 years pilgrims have made their way to Assisi, drawn by a tender promise of compassion. On a cold October day in 1943, Graziella Viterbi, a 17-year-old Jewish girl, found herself among them. The city of St. Francis did not disappoint her. Viterbi, her parents and her younger sister, were among the Jews saved from the ravages of the Holocaust by the Assisi underground, a network of Roman Catholic priests, nuns and lay people.

"It was the only place where they saved everyone," Viterbi says. "Not a single person was deported." The underground, now a nearly forgotten chapter of World War II, hid around 200 Jews in Assisi, secreting them in convents and monasteries and providing them with false documents, ration books, gentile names.

The Bishop of Assisi presided over the underground and his right-hand man, a young priest named Aldo Brunacci. Now 91, Brunacci looks back on those days as a golden, God-given chance to do the right thing. "Why did we do it? We did it because we had to," says Brunacci, who was later named by Israel as one of the "Righteous Among Nations," an honor bestowed on gentiles who risked their lives to save Jews from the Holocaust.

Jews started arriving in Assisi in the fall of 1943, after the German army seized control of Italy when its Axis ally dropped out of the war.

---

[1] By Candice Hughes, Associated Press. Used with permission.

'Hunt for Jews Was On'

"That's when the real persecution began," Viterbi recalls. "The hunt for Jews was on." The Viterbi family lived in Padua in northern Italy. They were vacationing in the mountains of northern Italy when the occupation began. "We couldn't go home. We were known there," Viterbi says.

They decided to seek refuge in an out-of-the-way place, making their way toward Assisi by car, by train and, finally, on foot. Shortly after they arrived, they ran into some people they knew from Padua, who put them in touch with Brunacci. "It was a journey guided by good fortune," Viterbi says. The priest provided them with a new identity. They became the Vitelli family from Puglia, a province in southern Italy in the hands of Allied forces. They learned how to make the sign of the cross. They invented a new family history. They boned up on Puglia's geography and customs. And they kept packed suitcases under their beds – just in case.

"Anything could be dangerous," Viterbi says. "The stupidest little thing could betray you. On May 15, 1944, the Nazis stormed into Brunacci's house while Viterbi's parents were there trying to arrange for other family members to escape. He managed to hide the couple before the Germans hauled him off to a detention camp.

Released to Vatican

The archbishop interceded on his behalf and Brunacci was released to Vatican custody on the condition he stay away from Assisi. But by June, the war was over and Brunacci was back home. The Viterbis never went back to Padua. There wasn't much to return to, even though the family had lived there for generations. More than 20 relatives had been deported to their deaths in German concentration camps. The ancient family palazzo was in ruins and there was no money to restore it. After seven years in Assisi, the family moved to Rome, where her father resumed his career as a university professor. She got a law degree, then met and married a "freethinking" Catholic. They raised two sons, the eldest now a prominent rabbi.

Then, when her husband died six years ago, Viterbi decided she'd had enough of big-city life. She moved back to Assisi, into the same apartment where her family hid during the war. She is the town's only Jewish resident. Now 72 Viterbi says she may have to move because the building needs major structural work. But she hopes to remain in the city that saved her, the city she loves.

"Assisi has always given me a sense of security."

FOOTNOTE TO ALEXANDER RAMATI'S BOOK AND FILM «ASSISI UNDERGROUND»[1]

Many Italian and foreign newspapers, as well as some books which claim to have carried out historical research, (for example, a book by the Italian-American Jewish writer, Susan Zuccotti, *The Holocaust in Italy*, translated by Mondadori Publishers, 1987), in exposing the work that took place in Assisi for the salvation of the Jews, have accepted without criticism the story developed in the book and film by Alexander Ramati, *Assisi Underground*.

The undersigned, who was the only collaborator of Bishop Nicolini during the years 1943-1944 in this task, feels it is his duty to declare that both the book and the film have completely distorted the truth.

To confirm this declaration it is enough to read an article I wrote in 1946, and a talk I gave in 1982 at the Sala della Conciliazione in Assisi on the occasion of the day dedicated to the Jewish people. Representatives of the Jewish communities of Italy, as well as authorities of Assisi were present in that hall, which was filled to capacity. It is to be noted that groups of Jews who took refuge in Assisi at that time, Alexander Ramati himself, and many citizens of Assisi who were witnesses to the events, were among those present at this conference. Every assertion I made at that time which did not correspond to the truth could have risked receiving an uproarious denial.

---

[1] By Don Aldo Brunacci.

Above all I am deeply distressed by the fact that Mr. Ramati's film seeks to attribute the merit for the saving of Asssisi to a Slavic Jew, while that is to be attributed solely to the labors of the then Bishop of Assisi, Giuseppe Placido Nicolini, who ceded to the German Medical Command (in the person of Colonel Müller) many of the religious buildings in and around Assisi for the establishment of hospitals, obtaining in this way an authentic decree from General Kesselring. With this decree Assisi was declared a hospital city which the retreating German troops were forbidden to enter.

The work carried out for the salvation in Assisi of Jews and others under persecution had as its only center the Bishop's residence. Father Rufino Nicacci, leading character of the book and of the film, had never officially been entrusted by Bishop Nicolini with the task of saving Jews. He had never entered the Bishop's residence in that period and never had any connections either with Colonel Müller or with prelates such as, for example, the Archbishop of Florence. He was never arrested by the Germans, and the German prison in Bastia Umbra mentioned in the book never existed. Many other details were completely invented by the fantasy of the author as well as by that (none less fervid) of Fr. Rufino, who was for a long time the author's guest in Israel during the writing of the book.

A recent detail: the contacts with Luigi Brizi for the printing of the false identity cards were kept under my indications by a young Jew from Trieste, Giorgio Krops. Recently, Luigi's son Trento was reminding me that on a certain day in 1944 I gave him 50 Lire and my bicycle to go to Foligno to make the rubber stamps for the false identity cards. The truth about the events which took place in Assisi is much more interesting than the coarse, unlikely and romanticized story which unfortunately was taken as true above all outside Assisi.

But this did not happen with the authoritative international magazine, *Reader's Digest*. When the book came out in the

English edition, Mr. Ramati made an agreement for a good deal of money for an insertion in that magazine, presenting his book as historical.

A first examination of the book produced a very clear feeling that it was instead just a novel. In June 1978 the European Editorial Office of *Reader's Digest* telephoned from Paris to ask me if I could receive a member of its editorial staff, Dr. Denise Pilkington. After a careful inquiry into different areas of Assisi, she could not but confirm the staff's first impressions regarding the book. Before she left we read the book together for three whole days. We did not find one page that corresponded entirely to the truth. In the meantime Mr. Ramati stormed me with phone calls from Jerusalem begging me to help him not lose the large sum of money that would have been given to him by the magazine. But I couldn't tell a lie. And so, to his great disappointmnt, the book was not published.

On June 23, Dr. Pilkington wrote to me from Paris saying: "You will not be surprised to learn that we shall not publish that book!" And she added: "Because only history is worth the telling."

In various articles written and in many lectures given by me, I have always striven to restore the truth about that glorious period in the history of Assisi. But the continual spreading of these lies convinces me even more that I must assemble and publish all the documents in my possession regarding the events in question, and this also at the request of many authoritative persons. I hope to do this as soon as possible, because only the truth deserves to be known. Moreover, on more than one occasion I have had the opportunity of bringing to the attention of important Jewish personalities I have met during these years the fact that this book does a great deal of harm to their cause, since such an enormous falsity perpetrated by a Jewish writer for the sake of gain, might make doubts arise as to the truth about what really happened during the Holocaust.

THE SECRET LETTER[1]

Don Aldo, you are an eyewitness to a key historical event: a letter sent from the Vatican during World War II to the Catholic Bishop of Assisi, Giuseppe Nicolini (Bishop of Assisi from June 22, 1928 to November 25, 1973) in which Pope Pius XII made clear that he wanted the Bishop to help Jews about to be rounded up by the Nazis. This letter, if it existed, would be a rare, solid proof that Pius XII acted to help the Jews during the period of Nazi persecution. We would like to understand better the story of this letter, because many say that Pius XII was not interested in the destiny of the Jews, that he was "silent."

This is the greatest falsity that could be said! The first president of the State of Israel officially thanked Pius XII for what he did. When I was in America recently, in Buffalo, a journalist asked me about the "silence" of Pope Pius XII, and I responded: "Let me ask you, what is better – to do or to say?" "To do," he responded. "Well," I said, "then let me tell you what Pius XII did for the Jews, in all the convents of Rome, in the Vatican and in the extraterritorial zones of the Vatican

---

[1] Don Aldo Brunacci with Delia Gallagher from INSIDE THE VATICAN at Assisi, May 2003. Used with permission. At 91 years old, Don Aldo Brunacci is a key witness to Pope Pius XII's intervention to assist Jews during World War II. Robert Moynihan and Delia Gallagher from INSIDE THE VATICAN went to Assisi, Italy, to question Brunacci about the day his Bishop showed him a letter from Pius XII.

– there were Jews hidden in all of those places and surely all of these convents, could not have done what they did without the Pope knowing. In the Roman seminary, where I was for seven years, there were 500 refugees, between Jews and those politically persecuted. In short, the clergy everywhere in Italy did a bit of what we did in Assisi.

But to return specifically to this letter, which you reportedly saw. When did this letter from Pius XII arrive? How did you come to see it? And how can you be certain it came from the Pope?

It was on the third Thursday of September of 1943. The Bishop called me to tell me about this letter he had received from Rome. Obviously I didn't ask him to show me the signature! He told me it was a letter from the Secretariat of State on behalf of the Holy Father.

I would like to go directly to the main point, one that has become contested: In her book, Under His Very Windows: The Vatican and the Holocaust in Italy (Yale University Press, 2001) *Susan Zuccotti, who says she interviewed you, maintains that you never actually saw the text of the letter from the Vatican to Bishop Nicolini...*

Ah, Zuccotti! Yes, I did speak with her. What should I say? It is true, I did not make a photocopy of the text.

Did you actually see the letter?

I did not actually see the text of the letter, but look, I was alone with the Bishop in the room, he held the letter up and showed it to me. He said he had received the letter from Rome, and he read what it said – that the Holy Father wanted us to see to it in our diocese that something would be done to ensure the safety of the Jews – and the Bishop wanted to consult with me on what to do.

So you never actually read the letter?

No, the Bishop read the letter to me.

Then, as Zuccotti suggests in her book, it might be possible that the letter was not what Bishop Nicolini told you it was, that he was in some way deceiving you?

(Brunacci laughs) Impossible, impossible. (Laughs again) It is not possible that Bishop Nicolini was deceiving me. I am certain of that. Look, we were alone in the room and he read the letter to me. It was clearly from the Vatican, there is no doubt of that. Not from the Pope himself, personally, but from the Secretariat of State. It was a letter asking the Bishop to do all he could to help the Jews, and the Bishop wanted me to advise him on the best way to carry out that request. In fact, this same order went out to many other dioceses in Italy. I have spoken with many historians, and they tell me that these letters were sent out and I think they will emerge in the coming years. I think many new documents will appear in the future, especially from the papers of Montini.

The work of Pope Pius XII was a majestic work, a work of deeds, not of words. Zuccotti doubts that Pius XII could have issued such an order because she is persuaded by the campaign launched against Pius in 1963. But that campaign has been filled with slanders and calumnies. Still, Signora Zuccotti is persuaded by it, and so cannot accept that this letter was sent out, and she has to invent the story that the Bishop deceived me to explain it away. But the letter was sent out. I saw it with my own eyes, in my Bishop's hands, as he read it to me. It was a letter from the Vatican asking the Bishop to take measures to help protect the Jews. And we took those measures.

Don't take Zuccotti too seriously. She cites the book *Assisi Underground* which is just a tissue of lies from start to finish.

I know what was behind that book. But she accepts it and cites it as a reliable source.

Why did the Bishop call you to see the letter?

Well, I was called aside by the Bishop after our regular working meeting, held on the third Thursday of each month. Two steps away from the chapel where the conference had just finished was a room which he called me to secretly. He told me he wanted me to carry out the request of the letter, which was to help the Jews.

What exactly did the Bishop say?

He gave me this job in the utmost secrecy. Not even the priests most close to me knew or imagined anything. Even to a person to whom I was most close, who was like a teacher to me, and saw me looking a bit distracted, I revealed nothing, because it was very dangerous.

The Bishop told me I had to help him with this work. We already had centers for Italian evacuees, so it was easy to hide Jews among four or five thousand evacuees. Those who had money, once they were given false papers, could even go to a hotel.

Anyway, during that time I saw the Bishop nearly every day. These centers for evacuees were located in the various buildings of the diocese and they were full. Sometimes even the young people of Assisi came to sleep there at night because in the morning the Germans rounded them up to make them work in the airfields at Sant'Egidio, between Assisi and Perugia.

In fact, 27 young people died in a famous bombardment of Assisi. I was the only one who went to collect their bodies with a small truck.

What was the political situation in Assisi at that time?

Well, in 1939 the Second World War began, but Italy remained out of it until 1940. I remember like it was yesterday the day we entered. I was in the study of my parish with the pastor and a professor. The piazza outside was packed with people shouting Mussolini's name, happy that he had declared war. We three were near tears, because we knew what the war would bring. Remember, Assisi was occupied not only by the Germans, but there were also Fascists who allied themselves with the Germans and became even more dangerous than before. Assisi was full of Fascist spies and we had to work in the utmost secrecy. The Fascists had a secret organization, *Opera,* to uncover traitors; they would arrest you if they heard you speaking against them.

How many Fascists were in Assisi?

I didn't count them. There weren't many but they were dangerous. You know, in a city this small, even a few bad people can do great damage! I remember one episode. I was in the cathedral and one of these Fascists came to find me because he wanted the key to one of the churches we had nearby to use for a German storehouse. I told him, I am not the boss of that church, I must ask permission of the Bishop. He began to curse the Bishop and put a gun to my throat. I turned to the German official and began to explain and the German lowered the arm of the Fascist holding the gun at my throat and said I must ask the Bishop.

What were relations like with the Jews in Assisi before the war?

Before the war, there were no Jewish families resident in Assisi. After September 8, 1943, we began to welcome them, but before that we were welcoming the refugees from other parts of Italy, who were fleeing their cities that had been bombarded. At a certain point, the number of refugees equaled the number of residents.

How many Jews were refugees in Assisi?

Unfortunately, I didn't keep any records at that time. It was too dangerous. But if I calculate that in Assisi we had one center, then another in Perugia with a parish, I would say a total of 250-300 Jews.

Of these 250-300, how many were taken by the Nazis?

None. Last summer I went to New Jersey for a conference with 350 people in a synagogue and I concluded my talk citing a Paduan professor, of Jewish origin, who said: "We will tell our children the story of Assisi, because all those who passed through were saved; no one was lost." The New Jersey newspaper that reprinted my talk entitled it, "No one was lost."

Where were they housed?

All over. Mainly in the guest houses of the convents. I remember taking the first family to a convent of German nuns. I am still in contact with the daughter of this family who lives in Israel. She sent me a book she wrote about the time there.

They were also housed privately with families. They needed identification papers in order to go out and especially to get food. Bread, sugar, everything was rationed. So we had to provide them with false papers, citing free cities in the south of Italy as the place of birth.

The Germans didn't catch on to the false documents?

They were very well done! They were made by a typographer in Assisi who had a manual machine. We gave each one a family name from the south of Italy.

You personally were involved in distributing false documents?

Of course!

How?

I remember once I gave my bicycle and 50 lire to the typographer and his son to go to Foligno to my friend who would stamp and wrap them. A young Jewish boy was in charge of keeping all the papers in order at my house so they would be ready for me to distribute.

What happened to the original Jewish documents?

The real documents of the Jews, along with their valuables and jewelry, were put in the cellar of the Bishop's house. The door was covered over with a wall that the Bishop himself had built with his own hands. The Bishop was a holy man and followed the precept *ora et labora,* and he knew how to do manual work. While he constructed the wall, I held the candle because there was no electricity in the cellar.

What happened when the cellar was opened?

All the documents and valuables were given back.

When did that happen?

After the war. A few times, during the war, I had to re-open the wall because some families moved. I opened and closed it immediately, always at night. I used to go from Perugia to Assisi by bicycle carrying documents to families that had moved. We made appointments at the church of Santa

Susanna in Perugia. I went there at night and slept in the attic with some of the young Jews in hiding and left early in the morning to be back for school at 8:30 a.m. To make it up the hills, I sometimes grabbed on to German army trucks and let them carry me up! Back then, priests often travelled by bicycle, so I didn't raise any suspicions.

Is it possible to visit the cellar of the Bishop's house?

Well, the house was completely redone after the earthquake. For four years, the Bishop didn't live there. The cellar area still exists, but it has been made into offices and cleaned up.

Just before the war ended you were arrested.

Yes, Assisi was liberated June 17, 1944, but I wasn't there. I had been arrested May 15, 1944, and was put in a type of concentration camp. Thanks to the intervention of the archbishop of Perugia, and the fact that they were moving the camp, I was able to escape 10 days later.

Why were you arrested? Did they discover something?

Nothing in particular; they were very suspicious but didn't have any evidence. They threatened to take me north but didn't have time.

Then you were summoned to work in Rome?

I went to Rome at the end of May. (Bishop Giovanni Battista) Montini had asked me to work at the Vatican in the Relief Office. The Relief Office took care of political prisoners so in a certain sense I continued the work I was doing in Assisi.

I remember once after celebrating Mass for some young people at the end of May, the police arrested me as I was coming out of the church. They accompanied me back to my house before taking me to the camp, and I remembered that in my study I had a Jewish university professor and his wife who were looking for another place to stay because they did not feel safe where they were. Fortunately, the police waited for me at the bottom of the stairs and did not come up to my study. I took my things and closed the door behind me.

I am still in contact with the daughters of this couple: one lives in Israel and is married to a diplomat – she called me just a few nights ago. The other is in Rome, and one of her sons is a famous rabbi who lectured, together with Cardinal Martini, at the University of Milan.

Do you remember the liberation of Rome?

Yes, June 4th, 1944, was the liberation of Rome and from the Relief Offices which were near the front of St. Peter's I could see General (Mark) Clark coming up the stairs of St. Peter's in his jeep.

I saw St. Peter's Square and the Via della Conciliazione fill up with crowds who had come to thank Pius XII. There were many Jews among them! The question of Pius XII arose after 1963, and no one knows why. For what reason did they need a scapegoat?

UNIVERSITY HONORS ITALIAN PRIEST FOR HELPING JEWS IN WORLD WAR II[1]

Father Aldo Brunacci, a canon of the Cathedral of San Rufino in Assisi, Italy, received St. Bonaventure University's national Gaudete Medal March 25 in Washington for helping Jews escape the Nazis during World War II.

"Don Aldo's bravery in the face of grave personal danger represents service to others at the highest level, that of selfless giving," said Franciscan Father Dominic Monti, interim president of St. Bonaventure University in New York state. Father Monti and the university's president-elect, Franciscan Sister Margaret Carney, attended an exhibit at the U.S. Holocaust Memorial Museum with Father Brunacci before presenting him with the award.

During World War II Father Brunacci helped house, feed, hide, and educate 200 Jews in homes and monasteries in Assisi. With the help of other priests, he arranged for these family members to obtain false documents that would help them escape. The priest also hid Jewish families in his own residence. On May 15, 1944, the Nazis arrested Father Brunacci and transported him to a concentration camp, but they never discovered the family hiding in his home. Soldiers freed the priest and other prisoners one month later.

---

[112] Catholic Online – U.S. National News, March 30, 2004. Used with permission. See also THE EAST TENNESSEE CATHOLIC, April 11, 2004: www.etcatholic.com/apr11/jews.

Israel awarded Father Brunacci the medal of the Righteous Gentile for his efforts. He has been recognized by the Yad Vashem Museum and Research Center in Israel and the Holocaust Museum in Washington. The Assisi diocesan priest is also part of an archival film project directed by Steven Spielberg that focuses on Holocaust victims and those who helped them.

Father Brunacci currently operates the Pope John XXIII house, a major retreat house in Assisi, and a bookstore featuring Franciscan and medieval scholarship. He is also a respected Greek and Latin classicist and author.

GAUDETE MEDAL AWARD
ST. BONAVENTURE UNIVERSITY
MARCH 25, 2004[1]

For the Jews in Italy, the Holocaust began in the fall of 1943, when the Germans took over the central and northern regions of the country. They established a puppet Italian government, the Republic of Salò, and began measures against the 37,000 Italian and 8,000 foreign Jews in their territory. Arrests and deportations of Jews were carried out with more than 7,000 being arrested and held in local jails and concentration camps, and deported to Auschwitz.

Without help from ordinary Italians, the Jews would not have survived, and no group was more helpful than the monks, priests, and nuns of the Roman Catholic Church. They hid the Jews and partisans in convents and monasteries, and in remote villages. They established underground networks to move people quickly from place to place, and provided money, false documents, and ration cards. Priests suspected of hiding Jews and partisans were treated with special brutality by Germans and Fascists. 170 priests were murdered in reprisals. In the words of historian Susan Zuccotti, the Italian clergy demonstrated great courage and compassion..."Theirs was an altruism that lay people may often expect from the religious, but that can

---

[1] Editors' note: Excerpts from the speech by Severin Hochberg, historian of the U.S. Holocaust Memorial Museum: see www.sbunews.sbu.edu/Gaudete. Used with permission.

never he taken for granted. In Italy, most men and women of the Church were a credit to their calling."

In Assisi, a town of 5000, at least 200 Jews, none of whom had any previous connection to the town, were rescued by an effort carried out by its clergy. While the initiative was that of Bishop Giuseppe Nicolini, it was Don Aldo Brunacci, Canon of the Cathedral of San Rufino, who coordinated the effort. Father Brunacci was assisted by Fathers Rufino Nicacci and Michele Todde, Mother Giuseppina of the Poor Clare Convent at San Quirico, and others in a network that gave shelter to Jews until June 17,1944 when the Allies liberated Assisi. Don Aldo ran a clandestine school for the Jewish children. He was arrested on May 15, 1944 and taken to a concentration camp. At the time of his arrest, he was hiding a Jewish couple in his own house. Not a single Jew was betrayed in Assisi and no attempt was made to convert them. Jews were able to gather to pray and to celebrate their religious holidays quietly in the convent of San Quirico.

Don Aldo wrote, speaking of the region around Assisi: "We were of course, in connection with other curias, for practically all the Italian clergy were working on similar lines as ourselves." Jews were able to survive during the Holocaust, with the assistance of local people, and of clerics such as Don Aldo Brunacci and his colleagues, who at great risk, put into practice their love and concern for their fellow human beings.

ASSISI PRIEST
HONORED IN WASHINGTON
FOR PROTECTING JEWS
DURING WORLD WAR II[1]

Ninety years old, alert and possessing a great sense of humor, Don Aldo Brunacci of Assisi, Italy, remembers the German occupation of Assisi, a world-renowned repository of faith and art, the way it actually was in 1943-44 and not the way it has been depicted in films.

The priest hid Jews in cloistered convents; he invited them to attend Christmas Midnight Mass in order to quell suspicion about their identity; he even taught them in the schools and when one died a natural death, he saw her buried under a fictitious identity which was later changed.

He was the Canon of Bishop Giuseppe Placido Nicolini at the Cathedral of San Rufino in Assisi and the Bishop's right-hand man. Together they saved hundreds of Jews as well as other refugees who poured into Assisi during World War II, looking for asylum. They had some help from Colonel Valentin Müller, a German physician, head of German forces in Assisi for nearly a year, and reportedly a devout Catholic who was forced to serve the Nazi forces; without Nazi sympathies, he apparently turned a blind eye to the comings and goings of Jews trying to escape under the guidance of Don Aldo and the Bishop.

---

[1] By Gerard Perseghin in: THE CATHOLIC UNIVERSITY OF AMERICA (www.catholicstandard.org). Used with permission.

Recently Don Aldo, the only surviving lead character in this drama, was honored here in Washington. He gave the opening prayer in the U.S. House of Representatives on March 24 and then on March 25 he was honored by the Holocaust Memorial Museum in Washington. He presented Sara Bloomfield, the museum's director, with a decorative tile with a Latin inscription.[2] He then toured the museum and visited with Holocaust survivors.

For housing, hiding, feeding and schooling hundreds of Jews in monasteries and convents in Assisi, the priest has been honored by the State of Israel, which gave him the Medal of the Righteous Gentile, and by the Yad Vashem Museum and Research Center there. He is also part of Steven Spielberg's archival film project focusing on Holocaust survivors and the "righteous gentiles" who helped them.

St. Bonaventure University in upstate New York recently honored the priest scholar with their National Gaudete Medal for his "service to God and humanity in the Franciscan spirit of compassion and sacrifice, joy and hope." The Franciscan-sponsored University brought him to Washington, where he talked about his experiences sixty years ago.

Though not a Franciscan himself – he is a diocesan priest – Don Aldo sat in his room at the Grand Hyatt downtown and talked about how he is a "Franciscan at heart." Speaking a little English, he resorted to Italian most of the time and was assisted by an interpreter.

Don Aldo pointed out that when the government fell in Assisi, the Bishop had to step in, explaining why the Bishop and his top Canon or aide had to take the lead in helping the Jews. Assisi is a small hilltop town that was fortunately not bombed during the war. As a result, refugees poured into this village-like setting where "people were sympathetic," said Don Aldo.

---

[2] Editors' note: *Pax et bonum! Peace and all good!* A greeting of St. Francis of Assisi that has become a summation of his theology and spirituality.

On September 8, 1943, when the Nazi occupation of Assisi began, Bishop Nicolini received, as Don Aldo said, "an official letter from the Vatican Secretary of State under Pope Pius XII asking the people of Assisi to do everything they could to help all refugees, in particular the Jews." At that point the Bishop called Don Aldo and showed him the letter and asked him to take charge of caring for the Jews. Don Aldo pointed out that Assisi has many religious communities there with houses of hospitality for pilgrims. "For the Jews the problem was not resources, but hiding their Jewish identity," he said. First the Bishop and priest got them counterfeit identity cards, so they could get ration cards. He recalled how one French family arriving in Italy got new Italian identity cards that showed they were of Italian extraction coming from the French colony of Tunisia in North Africa.

"The problem was the Jews came with books, Bibles, and so on which could identify them. Rabbis had liturgical garb," said Don Aldo. The Bishop's residence was large, so Bishop Nicolini, who was an accomplished stone mason, put all the Jewish materials in part of the basement and then with Don Aldo holding a candle, he sealed it up in a room. When the Bishop tired from his masonry work, Don Aldo took up the trowel and cement and worked while the Bishop held the candle.

Because so many of the Jews were put up in houses of hospitality, they had to be moved occasionally to make it look as if they were pilgrims. Italian guest houses also had to declare visitors within 24 hours of their arrival and registration.

At other times the Bishop allowed the Poor Clare community of religious women to hide Jews in their cloister which in those days was behind grates. "The Jews would dress in the habits of the Poor Clares" when they went for a walk outside, said Don Aldo. Even a baby was born in Assisi during the year of the occupation.

When a Jewish family needed their money which was stored away in the sealed basement room, Don Aldo got it, and rode his bike to nearby Perugia where the family was hiding. On the way back he got a ride holding onto a German military vehicle. "So the Nazis didn't know they were helping," laughed Don Aldo.

The priest, who was also a teacher of classic languages such as Latin, Greek and Hebrew, also taught the Jewish children. In his hotel room here, he told an enthralled audience how one of those young women, now in her 70s, visited Don Aldo in Assisi last year and brought her journal which recorded those days.

Don Aldo said no one ever applied pressure to convert the Jews to Catholicism. "The only (intention)," he said, "was to save them."

When he asked some Jews why they came to Assisi, they said that they "trusted in St. Francis," who was the most famous resident of that fanciful, art-endowed, and faithfilled town.

DON ALDO BRUNACCI DISCUSSES
HIS EFFORTS TO SAVE 200 JEWS
DURING WORLD WAR II[1]

Don Aldo Brunacci of Assisi is an Italian Catholic priest who helped save more than 200 Jews during World War II. His work began in 1943 in Assisi just after German bombers had destroyed much of the sorrounding countryside. While assisting thousands of Italian refugees who flooded the city, Don Aldo and other local priests also sheltered and fed Jews. Don Aldo is 90 years old. I spoke with him last week after he received a medal from St. Bonaventure University at the Holocaust Memorial Museum here in Washington. Through an interpreter, Don Aldo said the Nazi's brutal Italian campaign actually helped him save Jews.

Given those thousands of refugees in Assisi, it was much easier to hide a few hundred other people, in this case, Jewish. The Bishop and I created a committee to organize the sheltering of all those people.

There were so many homeless, hungry Italian Catholics. Why risk your life for a couple of hundred Jews?

Well, the answer to that question is simple. It is what the Gospel asks a Christian to do.

---

[1] By Bob Edwards, NATIONAL PUBLIC RADIO, Morning Edition on March 31, 2004. Used with permission. Don Aldo Brunacci spoke in Italian and was translated by Jean François Godet-Calogeras.

Those Jews who were sheltered by the Catholic clergy in Italy were able to practice their faith. Was that ever a question?

No, there was absolutely no question to prevent them from practicing their religion. They went through interesting stories like an elderly Jewish woman who died and they had to bury her. But they didn't do anything to look like they were practicing Christian religion. As a matter of fact, it was in the wintertime, so they were helped by that. They arrived at the cemetery and it was very cold, and so everything had to go very fast. Don Aldo said to the people at the cemetery: "Well, we already did everything before, so we just put the body in and that's it."

I heard a story that the Bishop knew masonry work and that the two of you were building false walls so you could hide documents behind them.

The problem was that with Jewish families, not only did you have to give them a new identity and an identity card but you had to hide their Jewish belongings. The residence of the Bishop is a big house, so they went in the basement, they had different cellars, and they put everything in there. Don Aldo was holding the candle because there was no electricity down there and the Bishop was laying bricks with cement. And then when the Bishop was tired, the Bishop would hold the candle and Don Aldo would continue.

There was a funny story that was circulating in Assisi at some point that the Bishop and Don Aldo had buried two Jewish people in that place.

We've heard so often over the years of charges that the Church was not only insensitive to the plight of the Jews but perhaps even complicit in what happened to them. What we heard today from the museum historian was that the Church was very active in saving Jews. Why is this story still contradicted by so many authors today?

In September 1943, the Bishop of Assisi received a very classified letter from the Secretary of State of the Vatican asking the Bishop to organize help to take care of all the refugees, especially the Jews. Don Aldo says that Pope Pius XII, who was pope at that time, did unbelievable things to save Jews. And as a matter of fact, there recently was published a list of church organizations, religious communities, who saved Jews during those years. Just in Rome alone there were thousands.

Well, you were arrested by the Nazis. Were you – how were you caught? Were you betrayed?

No, he was not betrayed, but he was suspected. And the suspicion became so high that one day he was coming back home and he saw the police. At that point, he had a Jewish family in his house, and it was really fortunate that the police just waited outside. So they arrested him outside and took him without realizing that there were Jews in the house.

Did you think after you were arrested that you would survive until the Allied liberation?

He was arrested May 15. Three weeks later, not even, on June 4, Rome was liberated by the Allied troops. He was not kept in Assisi. They wanted to move him north, which of course would have been worse, but they took him to Rome. And that was his salvation because then Rome was liberated.

We've spoken here today about 200 Jews, and of course with children, grandchildren perhaps even great-grandchildren, that number is much, much greater. Do you think about that? Do you think about the numbers?

Yes, he thinks of that, and there is no way he couldn't because he remained in contact with those who are still alive or their children and grandchildren. Not long ago there came a Jewish woman who is now 70. She was 14 when she was rescued by Don Aldo with her family. And she came and brought to Don Aldo the journal that she was writing in those years.

ASSISI, 1943[1]

It's the start of a new day in Assisi. A chorus of church bells echoes off the well-scrubbed streets. Flowers overflow from the window boxes, cascading down pink stone walls. The Piazza del Comune, the town's small historic center, is already beginning to fill with the day's visitors.

If Disneyland is the happiest place on earth, then Assisi is a close second. And it owes it all to its favorite son, St. Francis, Italy's larger-than-life patron saint. His "enchanting nature," as Pope John XXIII put it, "seems to hover in the air," attracting thousands of pilgrims and tourists every year. But during the Nazi occupation, which ended sixty years ago in June, Assisi attracted thousands of desperate refugees. For some it was life-saving.

I'm sitting at an outdoor café in the piazza with one of those refugees, Graziella Viterbi, a Jewish grandmother with a mane of short white hair and bright, engaging eyes. She orders Coca-Colas for both of us and with a thoughtful smile tells me: "Assisi's been my home for fifty-six years."

"My family name is from the town of Viterbo near Rome," she says. "We have been in Rome before Christ or perhaps when Titus destroyed the Temple." As she speaks, I can't help but imagine her as a girl in the innocent days before the war.

[1] By Edward Kislinger in: COMMONWEAL, October 8, 2004. © 2004 Commonweal Foundation reprinted with permission. For subscriptions: www.commonwealmagazine.org.

Graziella arrived in Assisi in October 1943, shortly after Italy's sudden surrender to the Americans and the Brits. Already angered by the Italian government's refusal to hand over Jews, Hitler had turned on his former ally with a vengeance. The Nazis occupied the country and the Viterbis fled Padua, the family's home for five hundred years, where her father, Emilio Viterbi, was a professor of chemistry and dean of the University of Padua, which was founded while St. Francis was still alive.

Emilio was an admirer of Francis and kept a copy of inspirational stories from the saint's life by his bed. Perhaps, he thought, if they could reach Assisi, two hundred miles to the south, they could find shelter. When they arrived, they found the SS, the Gestapo, and the Italian Fascist police relaxing at the Café Excelsior, the wartime name of the café where Graziella and I are seated. Unsure of where to turn, Emilio sought help from Bishop Nicolini of Assisi. He was "a loving man," she tells me, "like a boy in his enthusiasm, clever with a wonderful heart." He told her father: "There is no room left except my bedroom and my office. However, I can make do and sleep in the office. The bedroom is yours."

Graziella pauses as an elderly but sprightly nun hurries past our table carrying a bag of fruits and vegetables. She nods mischievously in her direction and tells me that Nicolini had already filled Assisi's convents and churches with hundreds of Jews disguised as monks and nuns. I laugh at the thought of matzo ball soup warming on the convent kitchen stove. She shrugs and replies that at the convent of San Quirico, "the nuns even prepared a dinner celebrating the ending of the fast on Yom Kippur," the holiest day on the Jewish calendar.

Others hid in plain sight. Don Aldo Brunacci, Nicolini's assistant, provided the Viterbis with new identity papers (the Bishop kept the originals behind a picture of the Madonna on the wall behind his desk) and found them a room in a local hotel. He also enrolled seventeen-year-old Graziella and her sister in the Catholic school he headed, where their teacher taught them prayers so that they could attend Mass and take the traditional evening *passeggiata* stroll between the churches of St. Francis and St. Clare.

The café check arrives Italian style, folded in half under a cup. We walk toward the Hotel Belvedere on Via Borgo Aretino, passing upscale boutiques along the way. I smell fresh-baked bread, olive oil, garlic, and basil. We talk about the years after the war. Graziella married a Catholic and their son became a rabbi.

She stops at a shop on Via Santa Chiara, one of the many stores selling postcards and ceramics. A hundred-year-old printing press sits in the front window. This, she tells me, was used to print the false identity papers that were provided by Brunacci for her and the hundreds of other Jews living in the city.

Graziella points out an apartment building down the block. Her family moved there fifty-six years ago after the police began making inquiries at the hotel where they were then staying. After the war, the Viterbis remained in Assisi, becoming the first Jewish family to live there.

Graziella thanks me for coming to talk to her but adds, sadly: "Even in Italy, few people know what happened." I want to say that they will, but only time will tell.

A PRAYER
FOR WISDOM AND STRENGTH[1]

"May the Lord give you peace!"
(*St. Francis of Assisi*)

Lord, merciful, almighty, Creator of heaven and Earth,
we praise You for Your glory
and thank You for Your love and protection.

We are gathered here today in Your name.
You have entrusted us
with the gift of leadership of a great Nation.

Give us the wisdom and the strength
we need to fulfill our mission according to Your will.

Help us never to betray our mission
but to do Your will
in respect and obedience to our own conscience.

Give us the gift of discernment
never to falter in our decision-making.

Lord God,
You have treated our Nation with great generosity.

---

[1] Editors' note: Don Aldo Brunacci offered this prayer in the House of
Representatives, Washington, DC, 24 March 2004, when he was awarded the
Gaudete Medal from St. Bonaventure University and an honored guest at the
US Holocaust Memorial Museum.

Help us to treat others
with kindness, generosity, and justice.

Give us peace of mind and heart,
that peace which comes from You.

Grant peace to our families,
to our Nation,
and to the whole world.

COMITATO CITTADINO DI LIBERAZIONE NAZIONALE

Cittadini!

Salutiamo i valorosi soldati delle Nazioni Unite che hanno combattuto e combattono per ricacciare al di là delle Alpi, insieme ai nostri patrioti, le orde naziste qui chiamate dal fascismo, e per ridare a noi la coscienza e la dignità di uomini, conculcate da un regime d'infamia e d'ignominia.

In quest'ora grave di eventi rivolgiamo il nostro pensiero ai caduti e ai combattenti di tutte le guerre, ai mutilati, ai feriti, a tutte le vittime della violenza fascista, senza peraltro dimenticare i fratelli dell'Italia tutt'ora irredenta, invasa e calpestata dall'odiato nemico.

L'immane conflitto, voluto e imposto da Hitler e Mussolini, si avvia fatalmente al suo epilogo. Le brutali aggressioni perpetrate nel mondo per soggiocare e sopprimere la libertà dei popoli sono fallite per il tempestivo intervento di tutte le forze democratiche e dei Popoli Sovietici, che riavutesi e organizzatesi, hanno preso l'offensiva su tutti i fronti di battaglia, per liberare e redimere gradatamente le Nazioni che il nazismo credeva già asservite al suo carro di dominazione mondiale.

Fratelli di ogni Partito e Cittadini tutti!

In quest'ora grave e solenne nella quale gli sguardi degli uomini liberi d'ogni continente si affiggono su di noi, nessuno osi turbare l'esultanza degli animi con propositi di particolari vendette e con atti inconsulti.

Chi è stato indegnamente offeso, reprima il generoso sdegno e affidi alla Legge sovrana la missione di punire i colpevoli. Mostriamoci figli non degeneri dei Martiri del Risorgimento e diamo inizio con severa disciplina alla rinascita morale e spirituale della nostra Patria che le permetterà di riprendere il rango di grande Nazione, conscia dei propri destini, in seno a una Umanità più serena e illuminata.

Assisi, dal Palazzo Comunale 17 giugno 1944.

I MEMBRI DEL COMITATO

ARTI GRAFICHE L. ZUBBOLI - ASSISI

CIVIC COMMITTEE FOR NATIONAL LIBERATION

Citizens!

We hail the brave soldiers of the United Nations who have fought and continue to fight alongside our patriots to drive back over the Alps the Nazi hordes called here by Fascism, and to restore our human conscience and dignity, violated by a regime of infamy and ignominy.

In such grave and eventful times, our thoughts go to the fallen and to those who have fought in all wars, to the maimed, the wounded and all the victims of Fascist violence, without forgetting our comrades in Italy, still unredeemed, invaded and oppressed by our hated enemy.

This unspeakable conflict, sought and imposed by Hitler and Mussolini, is inevitably coming to an end. The brutal attacks perpetrated around the world to subdue and suppress the freedom of nations have failed because of the swift intervention of all democratic forces and the Soviet Nations, which have recovered and organized themselves to go on the offensive on all battle fronts, to liberate and gradually redeem the Nations that Nazism believed were already enslaved by its wagon of world domination.

Comrades of all Parties and Citizens one and all!

At this grave and solemn hour, in which free men from every continent have looked to us, let no one dare disturb our immense joy with thoughts of individual revenge and rash deeds.

Those who have undeservingly been offended should restrain their noble indignation and entrust to sovereign Law the mission of punishing the guilty. Let us prove that we are the undefiled descendents of the Martyrs of the Risorgimento and, with strict discipline, let us commence the moral and spiritual rebirth of our Homeland so that it can reclaim its standing as a great Nation, conscious of its destiny, as part of a more serene and enlightened Humanity.

From the Municipal Building in Assisi – June 17, 1944

THE COMMITTEE MEMBERS

ARTI GRAFICHE ANTICA PORZIUNCOLA
S. MARIA DEGLI ANGELI - ASSISI

Finito di stampare nel mese di giugno 2005
presso lo stabilimento di Cannara (Perugia)